ON THE PERPETUAL
STRANGENESS OF THE BIBLE

Richard E. Myers Lectures
Presented by University Baptist Church, Charlottesville
REV. DR. MATTHEW A. TENNANT, EDITOR

On the Perpetual Strangeness of the Bible

Michael Edwards

UNIVERSITY OF VIRGINIA PRESS

Charlottesville and London

University of Virginia Press
© 2023 Michael Edwards
Printed in the United States of America on acid-free paper

First published 2023

ISBN 978-0-8139-5054-9 (hardcover)
ISBN 978-0-8139-5053-2 (paper)
ISBN 978-0-8139-5052-5 (ebook)

1 3 5 7 9 8 6 4 2

Library of Congress Cataloging-in-Publication Data
is available for this title.

Scripture quotations from The Authorized (King James) Version.
Rights in the Authorized Version in the United Kingdom are vested
in the Crown. Reproduced by permission of the Crown's patentee,
Cambridge University Press.

Cover art: Bee, irin-k/shutterstock.com; honeycomb,
Monory/shutterstock.com; sky background, Elenamiv/shutterstock.com;
gold background, detchana wangkheeree/shutterstock.com

For Raphaël, Éloïse, and Albertine

CONTENTS

ACKNOWLEDGMENTS

The chapters "On Eating Honey," "Paul on Life and Death," and "Heaven is Here" were given as the Richard E. Myers Lectures in Charlottesville, Virginia, on March 29–31, 2022. I am deeply grateful to the facilitator of the lectures and to Dr. Matthew Tennant, who hosted them, along with a poetry reading, in the auditorium of the University Baptist Church, and who introduced the first lecture. My heartfelt thanks go also to Professor Kevin Hart of the University of Virginia for his introduction to the second lecture, to him and his family for the warmth and liveliness of their hospitality, and to Professor John Dunaway of Mercer University for his introduction to the third lecture.

ON THE PERPETUAL
STRANGENESS OF THE BIBLE

Preliminary

Deep calleth unto deep.

Psalm 42:7

WHEN INVITED TO GIVE the Richard E. Myers Lectures, I felt
the need to descend into certain depths of Christianity that I
was aware of not understanding. I spoke of what was beyond me,
not as someone who, knowing, could instruct others. Perhaps,
having thought long and hard so as to have something coherent
to say, I may by the end have lessened my ignorance. Now, after
gazing on the borderlands of several mysteries, I see how much
is still to be discovered.

Each of the three lectures, and of the three chapters added
subsequently in order to complete their thought, is a searchlight
scanning the heavens, and we know that such lights illuminate
the obscurity only to a certain distance. My title could in all
seriousness have been *On Not Understanding the Bible.* And it is
the Bible that, throughout this work, I confine myself to reading
intently. The Bible underlies everything I have written, in English
or French, whether books of poetry or studies of literature, language, art, or philosophy, but it was only with *Bible and Poetry,*

first published in French in 2016, that I felt ready to make the Bible the single focus. Its writing confirmed, at least for myself, what I had long realized, that if the Bible is the word of God, our reading of it ought to be guided by two obvious but neglected facts. What counts is what is written; as with our reading of poetry, we should attend closely and exclusively to what we are given and not assume that a "meaning" or "message" is discoverable by paraphrasing, by translating what is said into our own words. Above all, we can only understand God and his world through what he chooses to tell us, all that we add being driftwood, and since it is God who speaks, we are always more, or less, out of our depth.

In the second excursion into biblical commentary, *Untimely Christianity,* where I was concerned to demonstrate that Christianity, however familiar and inoffensive it may have become, is always intrusive, alien to our wishes, foreign to our habits of thought, I mentioned several biblical passages that overwhelm our intellect, that shed a divine light so strong that human eyes see it partly as darkness. The present work takes up the challenge by looking, as into the sun, at an abundance of such passages. Hence its title, and my attempt, after having shown that Christianity is forever unseasonable, to show that the Bible is forever strange, forever leading us beyond its offerings that we understand to the further mystery that sustains them. While *Untimely Christianity* sought mainly to unsettle unbelief, the present work aims first to deepen the Christian vision of Christianity.

It proceeds on the understanding that theology is an attentive reading of the Bible, of the divine revelation perceived as inexhaustible. (So as to have the richest English translation to search into I quote the King James Bible of 1611, while referring to the original Greek or Hebrew where necessary.) I am also aware that it is a privilege to read the Bible, that to understand it we need to be given "ears to hear," that any true insight is an effect of grace. We are invited not so much to read the words of the Old and New Testaments as to listen to what is being said and to the voice speaking. Which makes one pause before writing. The Bible not being a rough draft for our commentaries, one is in danger of meddling, and of hearing awry, of getting in the way, of following one's own thoughts and falsifying the truth. I fervently hope the danger has been avoided.

The shape of the book leads further, by successive stages, into the necessary mystery of the faith into which Christians have been drawn. The opening chapter "On Eating Honey," worries at the relation between the exhortations in Proverbs and Ecclesiastes and elsewhere to discover joy in this life and the commandment in the New Testament to place one's treasure in heaven. The second, "Paul on Life and Death," plunges headlong into a number of jubilant, dark, and unfathomable utterances of Paul's, which may well have figured among those that Peter recognized in his second letter as "hard to be understood" (2 Peter 3:16), and which concern the awesome relation of the Christian to Jesus and to himself. The third, "Heaven is Here," explores heaven as a presence infinitely close, here and now, as an unmeasurable enlargement of the world in which we move. These three chapters scrutinize, with ever increasing wonder, the world as fallen. The final chapters, on "Seeing Revelation," examine the last book of the Bible as disclosing what is beyond our fallen world through a vision beyond our seeing, and as deepening the understanding, or diminishing the misunderstanding, of the inevitable strangeness of space and time. The whole book moves from the familiarity of eating honey to outlandish "living creatures," locusts like horses, a woman crowned with the sun, a city as high as it is wide.

The aim of the work, which endeavors to grasp numerous mind-stretching biblical statements and events, is not only to increase knowledge. The delving into Qoheleth's conviction of the profound rightness of eating, drinking, and being merry, or into Paul's providing the Christians at Colossi with this piece of information: "ye are dead," or Jesus telling the Pharisees: "the kingdom of God is among you," is not a matter of resolving certain exegetical problems, but of realizing how far we are from the heart of our religion and of seeing what we need. I continue to be amazed and unpleasantly moved by the distance that separates our little lives from the divine liveliness, joy, power, and single-mindedness of the earliest Christians, as one encounters them in the Acts of the Apostles and in the New Testament letters. What the biblical teaching studied in this book clearly shows is that we need to live at a different level: to descend lower, as the Bible leads, into the floorless horror of a world after the Fall, and to rise far higher than usual into the revolutionary knowledge of God in us and ourselves in God.

On Eating Honey

Jonathan . . . put . . . the rod . . . in an honeycomb, and put
his hand to his mouth; and his eyes were enlightened.

—I Samuel 14:27

I

I BEGIN WITH A COUNSEL among the "words of the wise" in the
book of Proverbs: "My son, eat thou honey, because it is good"
(Proverbs 24:13). At first sight nothing could be plainer; I had read
the words many times without any sense of puzzlement. As with
numerous passages in the Bible, however—and maybe, any passage in the Bible—one only needs to pause and read attentively
to become aware of being out of one's depth. The verse continues in the same apparent ordinariness: "and the honeycomb,
which is sweet to thy taste," or "thy palate." (We are reading
a poem, and that second part of the verse offers a variation on
the first—honey is good/the honeycomb is sweet—according to
the synonymous parallelism of Hebrew poetry.) One can try to
avoid further thought by hurrying on to the next verse: "So shall
the knowledge of wisdom be unto thy soul." It would be a relief
to think that this rather fleshly business of rolling honey on the
tongue, twice, merely served as a comparison to suggest how

sweet is the knowledge of wisdom; that one could pass quickly from the palate to the soul, from the sensuous to the spiritual. A comparison is certainly made, but the honey is present in its own right: the reader is not invited but enjoined to eat it and to savor its sweetness.

Nor can one allay emerging disquiet by telling oneself that the writer is doing no more than acknowledging the congenial things that accompany us in this fallen world, the beauty and life of God's creation, as also the beauty and life of human creations: what Augustine calls "the good things that God has bestowed upon this miserable life of ours" and that he depicts, in book 22, chapter 24 of *The City of God,* with unceasing wonder and Mediterranean exuberance. For our verse in Proverbs tells us to eat honey, and to do so because it is "good." It advises us firmly to delight in the world around us, whereas Jesus himself tells us: "lay up for yourselves treasures in heaven. . . . For where your treasure is, there will your heart be also" (Matthew 6:20–21).

Is eating honey, enjoying a fallen world, quite Christian? I have no doubt that it is; I don't imagine that I know better than the Bible, and the felt authority of the Bible excludes its contradicting itself. Yet a related idea, promise rather than instruction, finds me equally fumbling. It occurs in other sections of Proverbs, firstly thus: "My son . . . let thine heart keep my commandments: For length of days, and long life, and peace, shall they add to thee" (3:1–2). That obedience to divine wisdom brings peace we know, but the offer of long life seems frankly irrelevant, and far from the usual teaching that such obedience prepares us for heaven, which might be better attained by unconcern about living long. The theme returns: wisdom "is more precious than rubies. . . . Length of days is in her right hand" (3:15–16). And again: "Hear, O my son, and receive my sayings; and the years of thy life shall be many" (4:10). And again: "The fear of the LORD prolongeth days"

(10:27). The promise is not peculiar to Proverbs; it occurs in a psalm attributed to David: "What man is he that desireth life, and loveth many days, that he may see good? / Keep thy tongue from evil, and thy lips from speaking guile" (Psalm 34:12–13). If one is tempted to think, through disquiet, that one is dealing with the Old Testament and that, despite what Paul says of all Scripture being God-breathed (2 Timothy 3:16), one can take refuge in the New as somehow more authoritative, one then comes upon Peter who, having assured his readers that the end of their faith is the "salvation" of their "souls" (1 Peter 1:9), a teaching warmly familiar, continues by quoting the psalm: "For he that will love life, and see good days, let him refrain his tongue from evil, and his lips that they speak no guile" (3:10). He assures us in the same terms as the psalmist that we may love life rather than turning away from it with a view to the life of eternity. A similar passage that finds its way into the New Testament occurs in Exodus and is expanded in Deuteronomy: "Honour thy father and thy mother: that thy days may be long upon the land which the LORD thy God giveth thee" (Exodus 20:12; see Deuteronomy 5:16). Not only does Paul repeat this Old Testament wisdom for the Ephesians, "Honour thy father and mother . . . that it may be well with thee, and thou mayest live long on the earth" (Ephesians 6:2–3), he also reminds his readers that this is the first of the Ten Commandments "with promise" (v. 2). He recognizes the actuality of the text for the Christian by curtailing the quotation so as to replace the promised land given to the Hebrews by the more general "earth."

2

How does this relishing of life accord with denying oneself, renouncing all to follow Jesus, as insisted on in each of the synoptic Gospels (Matthew 16:24; Mark 8:34; Luke 9:23)? How can the desire for long life and seeing "good days" be reconciled with Peter addressing his readers in the very same letter as sojourners and aliens (1 Peter 2:11)? Or with the author of Hebrews describing the early heroes of faith as foreigners and aliens on the earth who seek "a better country, that is, an heavenly" (Hebrews 11:13, 16), and declaring famously that "here we have no continuing city, but we seek one to come" (13:14)? Or Paul telling the Philippians that our citizenship is in heaven (Philippians 3:20)? The fact that Paul updates the promise about living long "on the earth" (*epi tēs gēs*), whereas the author of Hebrews presents the faithful as merely resident aliens "on the earth" (*epi tēs gēs*), constitutes a particular challenge to one's understanding.

Should the Christian have a bad conscience about loving life? And if not, how do these various teachings meet in amity? I need to sidle up to a possible answer, and I begin with a longer look at Proverbs 24:13, where contemplating that incitement to eat honey *because* it is good lights on the fact that the Hebrew word behind "good" is *tōwb*, which takes us back literally to the beginning, to the origin of all things as we know them. As soon as God undertakes to speak the universe into existence, he sees that the light he has created is "good," *tōwb;* each of his successive acts of creation is *tōwb,* and he views the whole as very *tōwb.* The word *tōwb* has many shades of meaning, as does the word "good," and not all of its uses in the Bible have the resonance it develops in early Genesis or refer back to it. Here, however, the possibility of such a reference can be taken seriously. The sudden strangeness of the passage—the imperative: "eat honey," and of the reason given: "because it is good"—becomes intelligible if the simple product of the honeycomb is offered as a trace, in the fallen world, of that original world in which everything was good. Eat honey, not merely because you like it, but because it gives you the taste of a whole world lost but not entirely lost.

Once one has seen this far, it is easy to see a little further. What of the other, even more famous use of "good," *tōwb,* in early Genesis? We know that the forbidden fruit grows on the tree of the knowledge of good (*tōwb*) and of evil (Genesis 2:9); Eve's temptation finds an echo in wisdom's unexpected counsel in Proverbs. The serpent having assured Eve that she and Adam, once they too know good and evil, will be "like gods" or "like God," there follows a passage whose familiarity diminishes as one reads it in the light of Proverbs:

> And when the woman saw that the tree was good (*tōwb*) for food, and that is was pleasant to the eyes, and a tree to be desired to make one wise, she took of the fruit thereof, and did eat, and gave also unto her husband with her; and he did eat. (Genesis 3:6)

A first, small shock comes with the realization that the writer is not using the expression "good for food" in the casual way in which we might also speak of, say, weather good for walking. After the good that is asserted at each turn of the Creation, after the perilous tree of the knowledge of good and evil, to declare that the forbidden fruit was itself good is to ask the reader to reflect. The fruit was good as was everything that God had made. The tree itself was good, and the catastrophic knowledge of good and evil came not from the tree but from what was done to the tree, from the act of disobedience. Eve's fault was to perceive something as good to eat that was in reality evil to eat: to bite into the good with an evil intent.

Approaching the narrative of Eve's and Adam's fall with the honey of Proverbs in mind reveals the fullness of a curious parallel. Adam and Eve eat a fruit that is good; the "son" is to eat honey that is good. Eve wants the fruit so as to become wise; the sweetness of honey is compared to that of wisdom. (The words in the Hebrew for "wise" and "wisdom" are not the same, but their meanings meet.) Eve is roused to eat by the serpent; the son, by wisdom. The two passages when heard together clearly chime. They indicate that the writer in Proverbs is considering the very moment of the Fall and adapting it so as to suggest that the action of the "son" would be, as it were, a blessed version of the action of Adam and Eve, the acquiring of genuine wisdom through participating, with zest, in a good still present in the fallen world.

3

Another example of wisdom literature in the Old Testament, Ecclesiastes, contains a notorious and apparently troublesome passage that commends eating with equal warmth and constitutes a further seeming contradiction of the command to place one's treasure in heaven. In the course of what, according to our Western categorizing of literary texts, would be a dramatic monologue in prose and verse, the speaker in Ecclesiastes, Qoheleth, advocates mirth, "because a man hath no better thing under the sun, than to eat, and to drink, and to be merry: for that shall abide with him of his labor the days of his life" (Ecclesiastes 8:15). Similar expressions occur elsewhere (2:24; 3:13; 5:18; 9:7–9), each concluding with the same reference to "labor." It seems clear that the writer means what he says, and that, like the writer in Proverbs, he acknowledges the rightness of enjoying the world. Yet, in the same way that one might wish to spiritualize the honey that is good by reducing it to an attractive comparison for the taste of wisdom, Augustine (*The City of God*, book 17, chapter 20) disarms the threat of this eating and drinking by interpreting it as a figure of the Christian communion. I don't believe anyone now reads the passage in this way, but I mention the tendency to allegorize—on the pattern of those many passages in the Old Testament that we do know to have a hidden meaning because the New Testament writers reveal it with an authority that they alone possess—since it still leads commentators often to miss, for instance, the sensuality of the Song of Songs, with its not perhaps quite licit love, and to fail to treat honey and eating and drinking with due gravity.

This difficult matter—*can* eating and drinking be taken quite that seriously?—becomes at once more complex and, I think, clearer when one reads Ecclesiastes as itself a reading of the opening chapters of Genesis. It becomes more complex since Qoheleth introduces a second pair of opposites. The labor that continually exercises his mind is a result of the Fall, God having said to Adam: "In the sweat of thy face shalt thou eat bread" (Genesis 3:19). Hence, among the thirty-odd occurrences of the word in this short work, the very first question that he poses: "What profit hath a man of all his labor which he taketh under the sun?" (Ecclesiastes 1:3). Given that we suffer, as punishment for that primal disobedience, labor and, above all, death, and that the cycle of labor and death, like the sequence of the generations, the circuits of the sun and of the wind and the incessant flowing of rivers into the sea (1:4–7), seems to have no end, Qoheleth is clearly saying to himself, not "So what?" but "So, what?"—what does God expect us to do, forever, during our punishment? By commending mirth in the context of labor he opposes the enjoyment of the world to the fallenness, the "vanity" of the world. But how can one enjoy life, savor the honey of Proverbs, in a world groaning for redemption?

Qoheleth's search for the good is correspondingly more complex. The other result of the Fall is to burden us with the *knowledge* of good and evil, which do not occur, moreover, as clear and distinct ideas, being, in Milton's phrase in *Areopagitica*, "two twins cleaving together." Qoheleth acquainted his heart, he writes, with wisdom, "till I might see what was that good for the sons of men, which they should do under the heaven all the days of their life" (Ecclesiastes 2:3). Despite repeated discouragement, he disseminates the word "good" (always the *tōwb* of Genesis, on which he is meditating) throughout the monologue, often to let in shafts of light and to show his firm underlying piety, as when he declares that "Wisdom is good" (7:11), or that "God giveth to a man that is good in his sight wisdom, and knowledge, and joy" (2:26). He discovers an answer to his search in a fine sentence that constitutes a composite and thoughtful tautology: "I know that there is no *good* in (men), but for a man to rejoice, and to do *good* in his life. And also that every man should eat and drink, and enjoy the *good* of all his labor, it is the gift of God" (3:12–13, emphasis mine). The good is to do good and to enjoy the good things of life. It may sound simple, as if one should say: It is wrong to do wrong, but the writer is distinguishing, or rather, refusing to distinguish absolutely, between two kinds of good: the moral good that one does and the good, the pleasure, one feels in benefitting from one's labor by eating and drinking. The first "good" is sometimes understood as having the same morally neutral sense as the second, that of doing good to oneself, but the writer is using an expression which normally has a full moral sense, as elsewhere in the work, so as to play over two meanings of the word. (Early translators read the expression in this way. The Septuagint has *tou poiein agathon,* the Vulgate, *facere bene.*)

Qoheleth agrees with the writer in Proverbs that the good is involved in eating honey, in eating and drinking; that an original goodness is or may be present in the pleasures of life. How important, therefore, to retain the sequence "good ... good ... good"! Removing it by varying the words, as in most modern translations, effaces both the process and the fruit of the biblical writer's thinking. His genuine devotion—that of a man, one remembers, who continually cries "vanity of vanities"—emerges in the words that end his sentence and that express a kind of wonder at the relation between the searing narrative of the Fall and the possibility of rejoicing: "it is the gift of God." The cursing includes a blessing.

4

Proverbs—to return to that in many ways sister book of Ecclesiastes—has a more figurative approach to good and evil, and to placing its eating of honey in a fallen world. Its writers contrast the two terms by viewing honey from different angles—or, more accurately, whoever put the work together made possible the discovery of these differing perspectives. At one point "pleasant words" are compared to "an honeycomb, sweet to the soul, and health to the bones" (Proverbs 16:24). Both words and honey produce that salutary effect; honey is shown once again as being good for the soul as for the body. (That pleasant words can profit the body suggests that Hebraic sense of the wholeness of the person—with no Platonic relegation of body—which Christianity has inherited: "I believe in . . . the resurrection of the body," "This is my body"). At other points one comes on this: "Hast thou found honey? eat so much as is sufficient for thee, lest thou be filled therewith, and vomit it" (25:16)—through their happy lack of squeamishness biblical writers can give us reality uneuphemized—and especially this: "It is not good (not *tôwb*) to eat much honey" (25:27). The writer deftly shows the ambiguity of eating honey by referring to the case where it is "not good." Personifications also oppose good and evil. Against wisdom personified as a woman continually crying to be heard in the streets stands what the King James and other versions call "the strange woman" (e.g., 6:24), an adulteress or prostitute and in a quite other sense a woman of the streets. One description links her brilliantly to honey and to its spiritual implications. "My son, attend unto my wisdom . . . that thy lips may keep knowledge. For the lips of a strange woman drop as an honeycomb" (5:1–3). Poetry is at work here, playing in passing with the dissimilar lips and causing the counsel to eat honey because it is good to be colored by the realization that honey is equivocal, or rather that good and evil meet, that part of the definition of a fallen world is that our knowledge of good and evil is troubled.

So we have two questions to answer. Is it right to "eat honey" when told to direct one's thoughts towards heaven? Is it short-sighted to "eat, drink, and be merry" given our anxious knowledge of good and evil in a fallen world? The first is only partially answered by the fact that enjoying what is good is tasting something of the original good still present and requires further thought. The second darkens the more one explores evil and "vanity." Not only do we not know spontaneously what is good for us, because we have come by the knowledge of good and evil nefariously, by an original act of disobedience, but Qoheleth's searching of evil is quite precipitous. The King James Version for Ecclesiastes 1:13 runs: "And I gave my heart to seek and search out by wisdom concerning all things that are done under heaven: this sore travail hath God given to the sons of man to be exercised therewith." The word for "sore" (travail) is *ra', evil.* The translators' choice of adjective is understandable. It conveys, as would "grievous" or "heavy," a feature of the Hebrew word that Qoheleth no doubt intends. But in using a highly charged word, is he not suggesting that the search for wisdom is, deep down, an evil task, not because we should be wrong to undertake it, but because in a fallen world even that good task is affected by the evil that we have chosen to know? A few verses later he returns to this fatal knowledge: "in much wisdom is much grief: and he that increaseth knowledge increaseth sorrow" (v. 18). Even the knowledge evilly coveted turns out to participate in the punishment, by serving to illuminate labor and death.

This is powerful thinking, a deepening of our understanding of a fallen world that I do not remember from any other of the biblical writings. Qoheleth's celebrated refrain: "Vanity of vanities; all is vanity"—an utterance both repetitive and terse, slippery to hold and a true challenge to thought—is even more stark. So stark that many, including Augustine and Bossuet, simplify the task of understanding by limiting its scope. Yet the perception of vanity is not peculiar to this work; two psalms attributed to David share it in part. Psalm 144 claims that "Man is like to vanity: his days are as a shadow that passeth away" (v. 4). Addressing God, Psalm 39 echoes this and reinforces it: "mine age (better: my life) is as nothing before thee: verily every man . . . is altogether vanity" (v. 5). Qoheleth assumes the vision and widens it.

It seems to me that what he says is, from one of the correct perspectives on things, simply true, and that we need to acknowledge this so as fully to understand the welcome he gives to eating, drinking, and being merry. Certainly the end of his refrain, "all is vanity," sounds shrewdly final; one might well wish to rebel. Does he not take perfectly seriously, however, the disaster of the Fall? Does he not see that everything is shadowed by that wild act of disobedience? And what of Paul going even further, and stating that the whole creation has been made "subject to vanity" (Romans 8:20), while using for "vanity" the Greek word (*mataiotēs*) found in the Septuagint as the translation of "vanity" in Ecclesiastes?

5

I wrote this lecture in Burgundy, France, during what seemed an eternal spring of radiant sunshine, while delighting in the flowers, trees, nightingales and squirrels that peopled the garden and in the valley covered with crops and flocks and herds, and while often listening to major music. I was at home in the world of eating honey, of eating, drinking and being merry. I was not unaware, when looking up from my desk at the light-filled roses opening before my study window, of the acute contrast between a world of "vanity" and all that I was enjoying under the sun. I was thinking also that, if Qoheleth sees the sun as rising, falling and rising again in a kind of never-ending and inert repetition (Ecclesiastes 1:5), the psalmist sees the same sun as "a bridegroom coming out of his chamber" and rejoicing "as a strong man to run a race" (Psalm 19:5), and that he has a quite other awestruck sense of the sun's apparent voyaging: "His going forth is from the end of the heaven, and his circuit unto the end of it; and there is nothing hid from the heat thereof" (v. 6). I was equally mindful of the difference between Paul hearing the whole creation groaning in labor (Romans 8:22) and the psalmist hearing the valleys shouting for joy and singing (Psalm 65:13). I was persuaded that in a fallen world nevertheless created by God and bearing his mark these two opposite visions of reality are both true. Nor was I unconscious, in delving into what Karl Barth calls approvingly (in *The Word of God and the Word of Man*) the "critical negation" in Ecclesiastes, of the love of God as revealed in Christ and of the infinite nearness of heaven. The truth of vanity and the truth of Paul's "Rejoice in the Lord alway: *and* again I say, Rejoice" (Philippians 4:4) illuminate and reinforce each other.

And a closer look at Ecclesiastes takes one further, it seems, by revealing another reason for eating, drinking, and being merry. After almost thirty seemingly sad references to what occurs "under the sun," Qoheleth suddenly comes out with: "Truly the light is sweet, and a pleasant thing it is (in the Hebrew: it is good, *tōwb*) for the eyes to behold the sun" (11:7). The relation to the sun, the witness throughout the work of labor and evil, undergoes a complete renewal, a change of sign. And why refer to the sweetness of light towards the end of the text?—a text that seems to me far more organized than the wandering rumination presented by commentators. Is not the writer gathering together the threads of his thought as he alludes once again to the opening of Genesis, to the creation of light and of the sun in a world as yet entirely good? In drawing attention to the Creation, he recalls a few words from only the fourth verse of his book that one might have missed: "One generation passeth away, and another generation cometh: but the earth abideth for ever." The earth abideth: within the "vanity" brought in by death stands the earth that God created, as something to be found sweet and to relish. One glimpses the depth of the repeated injunction to eat and to drink, as to partake of bread and wine (9:7), the natural nutriments provided by the creation. And one sees the further reach of what is said of God in such injunctions: "that every man should eat and drink, and enjoy the good of all his labor, it is the gift of God" (3:13). Beyond eating and drinking, it is the creation that God offers us. So one can return to Proverbs, to wisdom's curious advice: "My son, eat thou honey, because it is good; and the honeycomb, which is sweet to thy taste" (Proverbs 24:13). The naturalness of honey carries within itself the whole sustaining creation. The word for "sweet" is that used in Ecclesiastes to describe sunlight. In the other similar instance in Proverbs of a honeycomb, the work probably of a different writer: "Pleasant words are as an honeycomb, sweet to the soul, and health to the bones" (16:24), the word behind "sweet" is the same, and the honeycomb nourishes the soul with the sweetness of the creation. As Ecclesiastes draws to a close, its considering of the creation explains the well-known words: "Remember now thy Creator in the days of thy youth" (12:1)—well-known yet maybe not well understood. The word for Creator is rare in the Bible (two other occurrences in the Old

Testament, two in the New), and is surely chosen so as to crown the thought concerning the creation. Finding one's well-being in the creation by eating and by mirth is perfected by a due reverence for its and one's own Creator.

On reaching the end of Ecclesiastes one might also remember another early statement equally unexpected: "He hath made every thing beautiful in its time" (3:11; the Jacobean "his time" in the King James Version is now misleading). I should like to believe that Qoheleth has in mind our responsiveness to each season of the year and to each season of our life and of the lives of those for whom we care, but this is speculation; the exact content of the thought still needs to be uncovered. What is clear is the beauty of *every* thing in its time, with the suggestion, it seems, that under the light of God's creation, the experience of mirth and the sense of vanity should advance in the awareness of that beauty and that rhythm.

The final words of Qoheleth, the invented speaker of the monologue, are nevertheless: "Vanity of vanities . . . all is vanity" (12:8). Yet the author of the work declares, in a phrase that startles even more than the others, that Qoheleth "sought to find out words of delight" (12:10; "acceptable words" in KJV is inexact). Occurring only two verses later, the phrase clearly implies that the author sees in his character's writing a profound joy of which eating and drinking are a manifestation and that is by no means overwhelmed by the equal truth of vanity.

6

Eating honey and eating, drinking, and being merry are at the heart of a vision. They enable an outgoing relation to the good, as it continues in a fallen world, and to the earth and the sun, to light and beauty—to the whole of God's creation and to its Creator.

And Qoheleth's equally visionary sense of vanity points the way towards answering my first question concerning the seeming conflict between this loving of life and seeing one's treasure in heaven. To enjoy life while yet perceiving the vanity of a fallen world is to be both "merry" and unsatisfied. Being satisfied with "honey" is mortal danger. Hence Jesus's warning: "He that loveth his life (*psychēn*) shall lose it; and he that hateth his life (*psychēn*) in this world shall keep it unto life (*zōēn*) eternal" (John 12:25; different words in the Greek mark the distinction between one's own life and life itself.) I note in passing that Jesus is speaking in verse, according to the parallelism—in this case, antithetical—of Hebrew poetry: loveth … lose/hateth … keep, since his frequent and spontaneous poetic compositions crown the important fact that the Bible as the word of God comes to us so often and so suggestively as poetry. Such hating of one's life, or willingness to "lose" rather than "save" it as in Luke 9:24, implies dissatisfaction with who one is and with things as they are. Loving one's life and wishing to save it would mean that one is satisfied and that—to take up the terrible irony of an expression that Jesus applies repeatedly to hypocrites (Matthew 6:2, 5, 16)—one has one's reward. His words ought to be equally troubling to any Christian whose life is happy and successful. The poor are more blessed than the rich because they know what it is to want.

It seems possible now to understand how Peter can refer to his readers as sojourners and aliens (1 Peter 2:11) and yet speak to them later in the same letter of loving life (*zōēn*) and of seeing good days, as of avoiding evil to that end and doing good (3:10–11). Having shown them to be merely passers-through, temporary inhabitants of an earth that is not their final home, he can safely appeal to the gladness they wish to find in this life. Their eschewing of evil and their doing good will witness to their lack of satisfaction, their desire for more, their eyeing of the inheritance that

Peter has told them from the beginning is "reserved" for them "in heaven" (1:4). The similar passages in the Old Testament likewise suggest a double take on life. When the psalmist urges anyone who desires life and loves many days to depart from evil and do good, adding that "the eyes of the LORD *are* upon the righteous" (Psalm 34:12–15), he too assumes that one can love this life while being fully aware of a larger Presence. The writers of Proverbs also assume that "length of days, and long life" depend on keeping wisdom's commandments (Proverbs 3:1–2), and—to return to a quite heady expression—that the very "fear of the LORD prolongeth days" (10:27).

And this is the moment to listen to Jesus's own reading of Qoheleth on eating and drinking. He delivers it in the form of a parable, that of a rich man who, seeing the prolific produce of his lands, builds larger barns and says to his soul: "Soul, thou hast much goods laid up for many years; take thine ease, eat, drink, and be merry" (Luke 12:19; the Greek words in this last expression are those of the Septuagint translation of Ecclesiastes 8:15). The man's own reading of the text is that, with sufficient possessions, one can rely on the future and enjoy oneself with no thought of anything beyond. The parable continues: "But God said unto him, Thou fool, this night thy soul shall be required of thee: then whose shall those things be, which thou hast provided?" (Luke 12:20). God quotes back at him, as it were, the many occasions when Qoheleth grieves for the fact that whatever one has acquired will be lost at death and will pass to another. The man takes Qoheleth out of context, with no reference to eating and drinking as being a gift of God, to doing good, or to God's judgement (Ecclesiastes 3:17; 11:8). Jesus as exegete offers a lesson in hermeneutics, in how and how not to read a scriptural text. In drawing the lesson from his parable: "So is he that layeth up treasure for himself, and is not rich toward God" (Luke 12:21), he invites one to understand Qoheleth's eating, drinking and merriment as finding their proper place in a life that, above all, lays up treasure in heaven.

As to that heaven, Proverbs—to return almost to where we began and to remain with the reality and the metaphor of eating—reserves a most pleasant, and poetic, surprise. The heavenly future is evoked by an image, which returns several times in the first half of the work as a kind of leitmotiv and which again *places* the relishing of honey. Wisdom is "a tree of life to them that lay hold upon her" (3:18). The "fruit" of the righteous is "a tree of life" (11:30). When desire is satisfied, it is "a tree of life" (13:12). A healing tongue is "a tree of life" (15:4). As the expression "under the sun" is unique to Ecclesiastes, the tree of life occurs only in Proverbs (and allusively in Ezekiel 47:12) between its first mention in Genesis and its last in Revelation. The Fall excludes us from eating of the tree (Genesis 3:22), the way to which is guarded by cherubim and a flaming sword (3:24). Writers in Proverbs offer obedient and generous living as a partial feeding on the tree, on the life which it provides, as far as that is possible in a fallen world and with no conferring of immortality. John perfects in Revelation their inspired vision, when Jesus promises whoever is victorious that he will "eat of the tree of life, which is in the midst of the paradise of God" (Revelation 2:7) and when he repeats the promise at the end of the book and of the Bible: the blessed will have a "right to the tree of life" (22:14). "Wisdom is a tree of life" is an extraordinarily powerful and suggestive idea, a spiritually and aesthetically satisfying link between Genesis and Revelation, from before the beginning of history to after the end, and a reference to eating that relates eating honey to the aspiration towards acquiring or becoming the true life that God offers.

One then sees that eating honey in the here-and-now of a world fallen yet created by God and resonating with his praise is the necessary way to a higher eating, of the "bread" of wisdom (Proverbs 9:5) and of Jesus as the "bread of life" (John 6:35). The physical, and indeed the sensual and the spiritual are perfectly at one in a passage in the Song of Songs, where the two human lovers seem to merge with Jesus and his bride, and where the man says: "I am come into my garden, my sister, *my* spouse: ... I have eaten my honeycomb with my honey; I have drunk my wine with my milk: eat, O friends; drink, yea, drink abundantly, O beloved" (Song of Solomon 5:1). The honeycomb here seems clearly to have a more ample significance, and the verse as a whole may be a glimpse of that "marriage supper of the Lamb" of which John is told towards the end of Revelation (19:9).

Rather to my surprise, the teaching now seems clear. It is through a proper love of life on earth, in the midst of God's creation, that one should desire the life of heaven, or more pointedly of the "new heaven" and the "new earth" shown to John, once again as Revelation is closing (21:1). It is precisely the beauty, the fullness, the "goodness," the mysterious divinity of the creation that leads one to want more, the marveling satisfaction that is nevertheless not satisfied. We want what we have, but changed, unimaginably glorified. We glimpse the supernatural in the natural, the transcendent in the here and now, the "new earth" in the earth.

And we can now read on in the passage enjoining honey, and understand, in the light of the foregoing, the writer's continuation:

> My son, eat thou honey, because *it is* good; and the
>   honeycomb, *which is* sweet to thy taste [palate]:
> So *shall* the knowledge of wisdom *be* unto thy soul: when thou
>   hast found *it,* then there shall be a reward [or better: there
>   is a future], and thy expectation (hope) shall not be cut off.
>   (Proverbs 24:13–14)

Eating honey, savoring the honeycomb on one's palate, leads to the opening of a future, to an imperishable hope that looks beyond life on earth to a life following God's "judgment" (Proverbs 2:6–8; 29:26). It is of course the finding of wisdom that procures this result. Yet doesn't the passage suggest, by the insinuation of its poetry, that eating honey in full awareness of the creation sustaining one and of the Creator's love and judgment is itself a way to that wisdom, and not a mere comparison? Eat honey, for its *goodness* takes you into an immense world, an immeasurable future.

For the Christian, that wisdom is Christ, and that future is made possible by the resurrection. Is it significant that after the resurrection, when he has entered the life beyond death, Jesus asks the disciples if they have any food, and that they give him some fish and a piece of "honeycomb" (Luke 24:41–43), which he eats?

And what of the strange *manna?* This "bread" rained from heaven (Exodus 16:4), which prefigures Jesus as the "bread of life" and which, gathered "daily" (v. 5), foreshadows the "daily bread" that we ask for continually in the Lord's Prayer—this manna, which Jesus promises to give to "him that overcometh" (Revelation 2:17) at the end of time, had, we are told quietly (Exodus 16:31), the taste of wafers made with "honey." Honey, the simple product of the work of bees, leads into the dark and radiant heart of mystery.

2

Paul on Life and Death

If any man think that he knoweth any thing,
he knoweth nothing yet as he ought to know.

—St. Paul, 1 Corinthians 8:2

I

PAUL IS A CHALLENGE to people who spend their lives thinking
and writing books. A dazzling intellectual, learned, ceaselessly
curious, extrospective yet searchingly introspective where
need be, often astonishing, at once eloquent and exact, he knows
nevertheless that ideas, beliefs, doctrines are to be lived. That
one's most important thoughts only have life if they concern the
whole of the person, of what one is, and if they illuminate the
nature and the finality of being human. He was the best kind of
intellectual and a perfect example for others. He was in no way
a researcher or specialist, though had Jesus not confronted him
he might well have become a *doctor of the law* like his teacher,
the prudent and impressive Gamaliel. He also realized that the
knowledge we acquire on earth is partial and impermanent: it
will "vanish away" (1 Corinthians 13:8). It's a humbling thought:
all those striking discoveries, all those original ideas. Knowledge,
like prophecies and tongues, like even faith and hope, will pass,

and only love survive. (It is right and righteous to wish to know, but already, if Christians loved as they should, we would notice a change.) As a thinker, Paul knows that thinking is a prelude and an accompaniment, not the thing itself.

On an apparently lighter note, it is also rather deflating to register that, over against our own often long and maybe numerous books, the surviving writings of Paul occupy no more than 115 pages of the edition of the New English Bible that I have by me, or 132 if one includes the Letter to the Hebrews. Yet it would be crazy to congratulate him, to call him, with John, the greatest Jewish writer after Daniel. He would be horrified by favorable reviews and the awarding of honors. Seeing this clearly enables one to measure the fallen world in which we are to such a great extent happy to live (we eagerly welcome good reviews and quiver at the news of being honored), and to reinforce the conviction that biblical writers are like no others and that the Bible resembles no other book.

I shall explore Paul's way of thinking by trying to understand a number of his statements that are probably beyond me. In the previous lecture the passages under consideration were not necessarily difficult in themselves; the difficulty came from trying to determine their precise meaning and to grasp them in relation one to another. The Pauline passages on the other hand declare their difficulty as soon as one pauses on them; they reveal a profundity of thought and experience for which we are probably not prepared. The difficulty in putting together various moments in Proverbs, Ecclesiastes, and other biblical works arises from the dullness of intellect occasioned by the Fall. The letters of Paul frequently give on to matters that bewilder by the revelation of a spirituality beyond ours, where what escapes us could only be reached by a thinking that is also a being. In the first lecture I could hope eventually to find an answer. In this, I may have to settle for pointing the way to answers that others more quali-fied—that is, more blessed—may find. Or to put it simply: I am not sure that I *know* what I am talking about.

I shall be doing spontaneously what is recommended by both Archbishop Cranmer and Bishop Bossuet. In his collect for the Second Sunday in Advent Cranmer induces Anglicans to pray that they may "hear" the Scriptures and "read, mark, learn, and inwardly digest them." There will be much inward digesting in what follows. Bossuet, addressing Catholic nuns in his *Meditations on the Gospel,* is equally expansive in his accumulation of verbs: "Fix your eyes on any important truth that seizes your mind and your heart. Consider, weigh, taste, ruminate, enjoy (*jouissez*)." I am not sure that either Cranmer or Bossuet would take pleasure in being thus juxtaposed, yet they both urge that living with a text, that slow penetration into its riches and recesses, which alone does justice to the Scriptures and allows them to unfold depth upon depth.

2

The place to begin is Paul's confident assertion to the Ephesians: "you . . . were dead in trespasses and sins" (Ephesians 2:1). "You were dead." The temptation is to read blandly the well-known words, to agree, and to comment to oneself that Paul means they were spiritually dead (which is indeed the case) and not really dead, whereas to be spiritually dead *is* to be really dead: the reality of death is separation from God. What Paul says, he means, and we should be shaken. His words do not apply only to certain Christians in Asia Minor before their conversion; they apply to our friends, our neighbors, to many if not most of the artists, thinkers, scientists whom we rightly admire but for whom the final statement is that they are dead. The word should resound like a tolling bell. The verse, with its repetition by which Paul charitably associates himself with his addressees: "we were dead in sins" (v. 5), changes the lights for us as soon as we allow it to penetrate. Calvin in his commentary looked clear-eyed at this human wasteland: "we are all born as dead men, and we live as dead men," before continuing: "until we are made partakers of the life of Christ." He prompts a rewriting of the famous first sentence of Rousseau's *The Social Contract,* "Man is born free, and everywhere he is in chains," as "Man is born in chains, and everywhere he is free in Christ."

Paul urges the Christians at Colossi in the same way to recognize exactly what they were before their conversion: "you, being dead in your sins and the uncircumcision of your flesh, hath (God) quickened" (Colossians 2:13). For the Romans, he places and generalizes the teaching: "through the offence of one (Adam) many be dead (or rather, died)," whereas "the grace of God . . . by one man, Jesus Christ, hath abounded unto many" (Romans 5:15). Here, the revelation of humans being dead since the Fall vibrates with the memory of the passionate exposé in Romans 1 of the wrath of God falling on human ungodliness. And an even higher authority confirms the harshness of the judgement. Jesus himself says to a hostile crowd: "The hour is coming, and now is, when the dead shall hear the voice of the Son of God: and they that hear shall live" (John 5:25). He is clearly referring, not to the biologically dead but to the spiritually dead to whom he continually offers himself. Each of these disclosures of the true condition of humanity is accompanied by an unveiling of the grace of God, whereby the dead are given life.

But what does it mean to say that people are *dead,* and not simply sinners, or unbelievers, or creatures estranged from their Creator? How are Christians to understand that before their conversion they too were *dead?* The word is huge; how can one ruminate and digest it? It would seem that, left to ourselves, we go through life as if spellbound, attending school, working, marrying, raising children, ageing, blithely unaware of the wrath of God, not seeing ourselves as "having no hope" and being "without God in the world" (Ephesians 2:12). Or better, godless, *atheoi:* even the carefree indifferent and the cautiously agnostic are atheists in the underlying sense of the term. Not to believe is not simply an intellectual option, an exercise of freedom in a world of choice. The author of Hebrews warns his readers against an "evil heart of unbelief" (Hebrews 3:12), while Paul tells the Romans that those who fail to believe are "without excuse" (Romans 1:20). Unbelief is evil and needs to be pardoned. And the "dead" are ignorant of the fact that the very world they inhabit is fallen—not only full of diseases, earthquakes and other miseries but fallen from its first estate. Paul, as ever, names with accuracy, calling the only habitation that we know as unbelievers "this present evil world" (Galatians 1:4) and describing our loss at its highest level: "all have sinned, and come short of the glory of God" (Romans 3:23). Humans come short (the verb is in the present tense) of God's glory; they are deprived since the Fall of the divine splendor that shone, presumably, around Adam and Eve in Eden. Part of their wretchedness is not to know it.

Paul reflects on death, on the deadness that people are, even more radically than Qoheleth in Ecclesiastes. Gazed at, the truth is chilling—and overwhelming like every truth that comes from that other world, eternal and divine. Yet as one moves with difficulty from recognizing the truth of Qoheleth's "all is vanity" to acknowledging the pleasure one derives from the abundant and variegated riches of the world, so it is perplexing to remember that Jesus calls the mass of humanity "the dead" while observing summer, or listening to an opera, or conversing with a lively friend. And one must not think, concerning this death, "Ah, yes, but, at the same time. . . ," if the presence of another truth is allowed to diminish the horror of a dead humanity. Human kindness, inventiveness, originality—all that emerges from God's image in us, from his Creator's creative concern for his creation, from the gifts he continues to lavish—in no way annul the omnipresence of living death. And the real shock comes if one switches one's mind to another biblical truth equally well known but apparently quite discordant. Paul not only tells the Athenians that God gives "life" to all (Acts 17:25), but even that "in him we live, and move, and have our being" (v. 28). The translation would be more forceful if it simply followed the Greek "in him we live and move and are." But for God, moment by moment, we would not be. Here is another paradox that the Fall forces on us: unbelievers are dead, yet they have a God-given life and, in a sense that I don't pretend to understand, they live "in" him. In a fallen world contraries are both true and, as Pascal saw, the Fall explains why. Unbelievers are "without God" (Ephesians 2:12) and in another perspective with him. Above all, one remembers, they are the object of God's love. He desires the dead to hear his voice, and he is incessantly active on their behalf. We are born dead and loved by the Creator of the universe.

3

If Christians saw unbelievers as dead, the strange appalling vision would certainly bring a new urgency to evangelism.

One might have thought that in turning from the gloom of seeing such death to what Paul says of Christians, one would hear the joy of the gospel—which is indeed the case, but not immediately. What Paul stresses beforehand, as the objective definition of a Christian, is that he too is dead. "Ye are dead," he tells the Colossians (Colossians 3:3), and although a better translation is "you died," the effect is equally abrupt. One does not often hear this flashing directness from the pulpit, yet Paul returns time and again to his brief announcement of the unexpected and inconvenient truth. He has already told the Corinthians that they died "with Christ" (2:20), thereby associating their death with the Crucifixion. To the Romans he writes: "if we be dead (if we died) with Christ, we believe that we shall also live with him" (Romans 6:8), a formula he repeats for Timothy: "if we be dead (if we died) with him, we shall also live with him" (2 Timothy 2:11). He thus completes the context for this weird supernatural death by relating it equally to the resurrection. He includes a further element for the Romans: "How shall we, that are dead (that died) *to sin,* live any longer therein?" (6:2, emphasis mine), and then adds the final touch (which is also the last straw), by informing them that "we are buried (were buried) with (Christ) by baptism into death" (v. 4). The Colossians receive the same revelation: you are, he writes, "buried with him in baptism, wherein also ye are risen with him" (Colossians 2:12). Christians are people who died and were buried. This is, one learns, what being a Christian entails, not as a choice but as a fact.

Certainly, the death that occurs to what Paul names the "old man" (e.g., Romans 6:6) is accompanied by the gift of a new life. Dying and being buried with Christ affords access to his resurrection. Without God we are alive and yet dead; with him we are dead and yet alive. But forgiveness could have been simpler, and it would have been had we—that is, fallen humanity—arranged it: Christ having borne our sins, God would have forgiven us and invited us henceforth to obey him. We see, however, that God's thoughts are not our thoughts, and that to accept the free offer of salvation made possible by Christ's death and resurrection we must ourselves die and be resurrected, for only thus *can* we obey God, by being thoroughly remade, quickened, endowed with an entirely new life. What is offered: to deny oneself, according to

Jesus's command as reported by Matthew (16:24) and Mark (8:34) and by Luke who adds "daily" (9:23) and even to lose one's life as urged in all four gospels, is far more demanding than obedience to the Law, as such obedience was inevitably and incompletely practiced. Except that, on consideration, to obey the law perfectly, as only Jesus was capable of doing, would also have been to die entirely to oneself, as Jesus did. God's demands are forever absolute, and rather fearsome.

Do Christians take seriously this statement that "ye are dead," or "you died," or does it almost disappear by becoming a doctrine to which we glibly assent while hardly noticing it? And above all, if we do focus on it, how can we come to grasp it? How can we see ourselves, imagine ourselves as dead? The more I ponder the idea, the more it escapes me. Or is that the point? Paul, after all, does not ask us to imagine; he asserts a fact: you died, you were buried. This death was not necessarily experienced; in encountering Christ and receiving, out of the blue, the gift of faith, I certainly had no sense that I died, or that a former self consisting of what I had been was buried. This was a teaching that I learned later—as did no doubt the Romans, the Colossians and Timothy. If we search the Scriptures for guidance, all that we discover concerning, for example, the Ethiopian eunuch who believes and is baptized by Philip is that "he went on his way rejoicing" (Acts 8:39).

What our experience certainly does tell us is that while we are, factually, "dead to sin" (Romans 6:2), sin is not at all dead in us, as Paul himself famously knew and confessed with anguish in the same Letter to the Romans: "For the good that I would I do not: but the evil which I would not, that I do" (Romans 7:19). The emotion that works in him works also his Greek. The English translators of 1611 (as Wycliffe and Tyndale before them in a different order) capture the pain of his self-study in a sentence that advances through weighty monosyllables (only "evil" is disyllabic)—in a passage where monosyllables abound—and through words drawn exclusively from the Anglo-Saxon word hoard, from the Germanic wealth within English on which Shakespeare's characters also call when they reach a depth of thought or emotion (Lear of Cordelia: "I did her wrong"; Macbeth: "She should have died hereafter;/ There would have been a time for such a word"; Hamlet: "To be or not to be"). Perhaps Paul implies that, having once seized the fact of our unregenerate "I" being dead and buried, as something that God himself has wrought in us and as a factor in our relation to him, this should become more and more true in our lives, not by our reflecting on this death and struggling to understand it but by living according to the risen life of Christ to which Paul also refers on each occasion. Perhaps being really dead to self resembles humility in that one could only attain it by concentrating on something else, on whatever one should be doing or being. As one could only attain self-forgetfulness by forgetting the self. Perhaps, finally, all is said in the continuation of Colossians 3:3 that I only began to quote: you died "and your life is hid with Christ in God." It is in God's eyes, in Reality as God sees it, that we died and were buried, so that now our Real life is hidden in God, whether we acknowledge it or not. This is in every way a beautiful sentence, another sequence of wondering monosyllables in the English translation, conveying a meaning sublimely mysterious that one could spend one's life contemplating. Within a thought of death, a truth to make one glad.

4

A further way of approaching this enigmatic death may be the sounding of a Pauline statement in 2 Corinthians, which turns out, however, to be another passage that itself passes understanding. The King James Version translates it thus: "if any man be in Christ, he is a new creature: old things are passed away; behold, all things are become new" (2 Corinthians 5:17). The scope of Paul's utterances is frequently immense; here, in the twinkling of a sentence, everything is changed, from the individual to the universe. The first part reads in the Greek, *ei tis en christō, kainē ktisis,* or, word for word: if anyone (is) in Christ, new creation. The absence of a linking syntax before *new creation* leads translators to choose either *he* is a new creation (or creature) or *there* is a new creation. But Paul is not being vague or ambiguous. Neither the King James Version nor any other that I have seen does justice, as I understand it, to his searching ellipsis. One should surely translate it as: If anyone is in Christ—new creation, so as to show that in becoming oneself a new creation one sees the whole of reality as created anew. One is thoroughly new in a thoroughly new world. Here at least I know what I'm talking about, since such was precisely what I felt in becoming a Christian, and the realization has steadily grown. It is as if, as well as being converted oneself, the whole of creation was converted into what it should be—and into what, in God's eyes, it already is.

The excitement of Paul's sentence increases as one continues to read. The worst translations of the beginning lose the force of *kainē ktisis,* a new creation, by paraphrasing it: "a new person," "a new being," presumably with a view to a user-friendly text that makes the expression "understandable." But it occurs elsewhere in Paul: "in Christ Jesus neither circumcision availeth any thing, nor uncircumcision, but a new creature (or new creation, *kainē ktisis"* Galatians 6:15), and the words in 2 Corinthians are amplified by the context in which they are placed. As one reads on: "old things are passed away; behold, all things are become new (*gegonen kaina*)," one realizes that Paul may well be thinking of the original Creation in Genesis as rendered in the Greek of the Septuagint. When God said, "Let there be light," light "was," *egeneto,* and the word returns for the coming into being of "evening," "morning" and so on throughout the six days. In writing *gegonen kaina,* is not Paul thinking that, old things having passed away, new things have *become, are,* as in a new act of creation? As Christ the Word was the Maker of the original creation—"All things were made (came into being, *egeneto*) by him," says John (John 1:3), who is clearly rewriting the beginning of Genesis in terms of a new revelation—so he is the Maker of the new creation.

Paul sets no limits on the new, and neither should we. In his eloquent and learned commentary on 2 Corinthians, Charles Hodge, the famous nineteenth-century director of Princeton Theological Seminary, ventures a description of the change: "Old opinions, views, plans, desires, principles and affections are passed away; new views of truth, new principles, new apprehensions of the destiny of man, and new feelings and purposes fill and govern the soul." The largeness of the writing is nevertheless restrictive; the rather Victorian analysis concerns essentially the inner life. Yet everything is new. People are different, each person is seen in a changed light, each encounter is charged with infinity. Think of Jesus's meetings with people in the gospels: they are never ordinary. All of experience is transformed, including areas we might have thought not to be concerned as being spiritually neutral. How do we respond, for instance, to a late Schubert piano sonata? As before, in a sense: with the same concentration, the same openness of all we are to what we hear, the same sense of the mind and the body living more fully, with greater awareness and through transfigured time. With the same wonder at being elsewhere, while the music lasts. Yet, if what Paul also calls the "new man" in us (Ephesians 4:24; Colossians 3:10) is doing the listening, our appreciation, and the music itself, are new. Our humility before genius and the fruit of genius is more genuine, if we have learnt to be still and to know that God is God (Psalm 46:10) and to recognize that others are better than ourselves (Philippians 2:3). The beauty that we hear takes on a new meaning, as the prodigious hint of a heavenly beauty to come, such that our elation is also a longing and our joy is touched with the Christian sadness at not having access, here and now, to what the music promises. And we can listen "in Christ." We can listen with him, being thankful, and wondering, perhaps, what will be the final destination of the work, as of the *Odyssey* or the Rembrandt self-portraits.

What surrounds us bears the clearest stamp of the new. "Nature" becomes the creation: to the ears and eyes of faith all creatures praise God, from the stars to hills, to beasts and birds, to hail and snow (Psalm 148). To become new and to see everything as new is to glimpse something of the "new heavens" and "new earth" (revealed in Isaiah 65:17, reconfirmed in 2 Peter 3:13, and seen in a vision by John in Revelation 21:1) to which we pay so little attention. For "new" is a great word in the Bible, being charged with the whole promise of an as yet unimaginable world to supersede, or to arise from, the world disfigured by the Fall. Everywhere is touched with the coming newness, and God liberally accords us hints of the future. A gap in the summer trees at the end of our garden in Burgundy gives onto an orchard so suffused with a further light laid on the grass that it seems to be elsewhere and invites one to enter.

According to Ecclesiastes 1:9, "there is no new thing under the sun." According to the New Testament, if I may follow the Hebrew writers in making the pun richly meaningful, everything is new under the Son.

5

"If anyone is in Christ—new creation; old things are passed away—look: everything is new." It is one of the most exhilarating verses in Scripture. And here's the beginning of another: "For to me to live is Christ" (Philippians 1:21). These few words take us even further into the human mystery of Christianity. On top of appearing quite as unfathomable as the others on which I have ventured to comment—as well as challenging our understanding—they challenge our honesty. Would it be derogatory, or simply true, to suggest that many if not most Christians would be unable to say them with an untroubled conscience, and that if to do so were what Jesus defined as the qualification for acting, the woman taken in adultery would depart unstoned? Clearsightedness would lead us to say, "To me to live is me." In the race to catch my attention, Christ comes a poor second to myself.

The words form part of a superb sentence, throbbing with concision and power. Maybe one should begin by reading it in context. Paul rejoices in the fact that Jesus is everywhere preached, and he continues: "I know that this shall turn to my salvation through your prayer, and the supply of the spirit of Jesus Christ, according to my earnest expectation and my hope, that in nothing I shall be ashamed, but that with all boldness, as always, so now also Christ shall be magnified in my body, whether it be by life, or by death. For to me to live is Christ, and to die is gain" (vv. 19–21). The packed final sentence, which completes the confronting of life and death (and completes also in the English translation a sequence of nineteen monosyllables), follows, as in the Greek original, a very long sentence. Does this matter? It does: if, in the Greek or the King James English, you follow the rhythm you find the sense. Paul may be working up to this climax so as to state the fundamental definition of his life as he has known it for some time, but even if this is so, does one not sense his wonder as he finds himself expressing and contemplating the singular fact? For it may be that, as he reaches down into his experience, he partly discovers the truth about himself as he formulates it. This is, after all, what writing is for, at its best: to hit upon exactly what one has to say but did not necessarily realize one had it to say.

The sentence is even more succinct in the Greek, which can often dispense with the verb *to be:* "For to me to live—Christ, and to die—gain." We find no difficulty in saying that for the Christian Christ must be the center of his or her life. The problem, as the starkness of Paul's affirmation sinks in, is to apprehend the consequence of that absolute priority. The consequence was clearer—though in no way easier—for Paul than for most of us: his mission was to preach Christ and everything in his life had to be oriented to that end. Yet the demand he made of himself corresponds to the sovereign, exclusive demand that God imposes on all who worship him. The commandment that Moses gives in Deuteronomy 6:5 and that Jesus calls "the first and great commandment" (Matthew 22:38; Mark 12:29–30) is: "thou shalt love the Lord thy God" and do so, moreover, "with all thine heart, and with all thy soul, and with all thy might." Not only is our first duty to love God, but the whole of our being should be engaged in that single pursuit. The words are familiar; the practice maybe a little less so. Some even better-known words imply the same singular commitment. The first thing we find ourselves wishing in the Lord's Prayer is that our Father's name should be hallowed, as in heaven, so on earth. The words apparently caused ecstasy and action in Loyola; we probably murmur them and pass on to "Thy kingdom come." Each time we say the prayer we declare nevertheless that our first and supreme desire is that God's name be hallowed, everywhere on earth as unceasingly in heaven, that everyone acknowledge and glorify him. Paul's hardly graspable assertion is no more dizzyingly exigent than these other biblical sayings to which we have become rather cozily accustomed.

We might make some progress in understanding by noting that those modern translations that have Paul say: "to me life is Christ" rather than "to live is Christ," although right in suggesting the all-encompassing scope of his statement, miss the active, existential purport of "to live." One might even better translate: "to me living is Christ," the force of the so valuable English gerund lending itself perfectly to continuous and energetic acting through time. We meet here what seems to me the Hebraic sense of the person, of *being* (another gerund) as an active process involving all that one is. Truth in the Bible is not an abstraction: it is something one does. "He that doeth truth," says John (*ho de poiōn tēn alētheian*) "cometh to the light" (John 3:21). He warns in his first letter that if we say we have fellowship with God and yet walk in darkness we lie, "and do not the truth" (*kai ou poioumen tēn alētheian,* 1 John 1:6). In his third letter he speaks twice of walking in truth (*kathōs sy en alētheia peripateis . . . ta ema tekna en tē alētheia peripatounta,* 3 John 3–4). Similarly, faith is not a Western-style assent to doctrine. "For in Jesus Christ neither circumcision availeth any thing, nor uncircumcision," Paul writes to the Galatians, "but faith which worketh (*energoumenē*) by love" (Galatians 5:6). He thus opposes the works of faith, which justify, to the works (*ergōn*) of the law which he has declared in the same letter (2:16) to be incapable of justifying. If to live is Christ, one is engaged in living truth, in living faith, in living each moment almost as if one were Christ, the bond is so intimate. That may sound overstated, yet in the same Letter to the Philippians Paul speaks of a strange mingling of the human and the divine in a well-known paradox: "work out [*katergazesthe*] your own salvation with fear and trembling. For it is God which worketh [*energōn*] in you both to will and to do [to work, *energein*] of his good pleasure" (Philippians 2:12–13). God works in us, yet it is also we who work. Paul could have juxtaposed the two parts of the paradox: work out your salvation; God is working in you. By connecting them in the word "for," he tightens the enigma: the very reason you should work is that God in you is not only making it possible for you to work but is giving you the desire to do so.

On the Perpetual Strangeness of the Bible

The more God descends into us to save us, the more it is we who work out our salvation. The more, for Paul, to live is Christ, the more it is Paul who lives. The *less* one is, the more one *is*.

Which may be the further thought beneath the end of the sentence: "and to die is gain." The first meaning is clear. In living Christ on earth we know that we cannot fully grasp him, because of our sinfulness and his own absent presence, whereas in heaven we shall finally be with him, "we shall see him," as John writes, "as he is" (I John 3:2). The underlying meaning is surely that, in heaven, the new life that Paul lives will be really and entirely Christ, and that, as a perfected son of God he will at last be the "new man" that his spirit longs to become. Reading Proverbs and Ecclesiastes suggested that the very beauty of life here and now amid God's creation both satisfies and dissatisfies, and so creates the desire for more, for a new earth arising from the old. From the New Testament one learns a more fundamental reason for placing one's treasure in heaven, which is, of course, that one wants to be with Christ. Christ who, being God, is so many things, is also the link between loving life and hoping for heaven. The more Paul finds that to live, here on earth, is Christ, and that one should rejoice and rejoice again in him in the present, the more he longs for the future and to be with him in heaven.

6

Paul's benthic statements, which become progressively more challenging to the mind and ever more ungraspable as fact, lead me to think that I should be spending less effort in mulling them over than in trying to live in accordance with them. Everything I say is from a great and hardly forgivable distance. I remember T. S. Eliot in *Ash-Wednesday* stepping back from the poem and from thinking, praying that he might forget matters that with himself he too much discusses and too much explains. The unusual, rather Germanic order of the words captures his raveled anxiety at maybe losing himself in elucubration. I remember also the simple words of Proverbs 11:2: "with the lowly is wisdom." I sometimes feel that I am finding my way with great earnestness and expenditure of thought to what many devout uncomplicated Christians may know by experience.

Certainly, "to live is Christ, to die gain" perfectly summarizes the proper stand and conduct of the Christian. And Paul completes and intensifies the thought (and had already done so) in Galatians 2:20 by declaring that, having been crucified with Christ, "I live; yet not I [better: I no longer live], but Christ liveth in me." Of all the Pauline expressions into which I have been peering this is the most alarming, exalting, and mysterious. One can at least say that, were this true of all Christians, the world would be transfigured, and that our failure to make it true is unrighteous.

I have already explored the verse in the chapter "Not I" in *Of Making Many Books* (Macmillan, 1990), but there is so much more to find. For a start, to discover that Christ lives in one is to discern most clearly and at the deepest level what Christianity teaches yet many neglect. The object of faith has become the subject. Not only is Christ the Person to whom one relates by faith rather than simply the object of faith, the focus of a cluster of doctrines, but the relation is so intimate that "my" life is that of Jesus, and Jesus occupies the place where "I" was used to seeing myself. Yet having written that he no longer lives and that Christ lives in him, Paul continues: "and the life which I now live. . . ." He clearly intends his readers or hearers to be startled by this syntactic oxymoron: I no longer live/I live, and one also sees that even if the "I" that gives way is the "old man" and the "I" that lives now is the "new man," a further, unsoundable and sublime contradiction appears in the fact that what lives in him is both Christ and himself. John will record similar and equally mysterious sayings of Jesus: "Peace I leave with you, my peace I give unto you" (John 14:27) and "These things have I spoken unto you, that my joy might remain in you, and that your joy might be full" (15:11). *Our* joy and *our* peace are at the same time the very joy and peace of Jesus. We should no doubt also understand in this double perspective the nine fruits of the Spirit, beginning with love, joy and peace, which Paul identifies later in Galatians (5:22–23). They are our fruits but they come from the Spirit. What he confers is a divine love, a divine joy, a divine peace different in kind from the human versions we are capable of producing ourselves.

It is also significant that the person who sees himself as effaced (and yet not effaced) by Christ remains the most vivid and angular personality of the New Testament.

Paul's determination to be a place where Christ lives echoes the aspiration of John the Baptist: "He must increase, but I must decrease" (John 3:30), and above all, though at a quite different level, Jesus's knowledge of his oneness with the Father—"I and my Father are one" (John 10:30)—and of their dwelling the one in the other: "the Father is in me, and I in him" (v. 38). Paul exclaims that "Christ liveth in me," and Jesus proclaims "The Father is in me": we are clearly on hallowed ground, and we must be content with whatever understanding we are given. And there is more. Writing to the Ephesians, Paul recounts his prayer to God on their behalf:

> That he would grant you, according to the riches of his glory, to be strengthened with might by his Spirit in the inner man;
> That Christ may dwell in your hearts by faith; that ye, being rooted and grounded in love,
> May be able to comprehend with all saints what *is* the breadth, and length, and depth, and height;

And to know the love of Christ, which passeth knowledge,
that ye might be filled with all the fullness of God.
(Ephesians 3:16–19)

The power of the writing (a single sentence that must be kept
in translation) and of the immense divine world that opens up
before and around the reader convey progressively, through the
references to the Spirit, to Christ and to God, the presence here
and now of what the Bible abstains from calling the Trinity, and
Paul's desire that no less than the Trinity dwell in us. The sentence culminates in Paul's realization of the outlandishness of
such a possibility through the dense rhetoric of the conclusion.
He prays that the Ephesians—and the Bible prays, as it were, that
all Christians—may know (*gnōnai*) a love that surpasses knowledge (*tēs gnōseōs*), the paradox of knowing what is unknowable
revealing clearly the infinite distance between our grasp and all
there is to be grasped. (The paradox strikes even more readily
in the Greek, which says: to know surpassing-knowledge love.)
The final words, "that ye might be filled (*plērōthēte*) with all the
fullness (*plērōma*) of God," emphasize the fullness of this filling
by a kind of variant of the cognate accusative, to the point that
our marveling at being filled with God seizes at the same time the
impossibility of his infinite fullness entering our own finitude.
The two final parts of the sentence seem to work together in
order to suggest that, as we can know Christ's beyond-knowledge
love only in keeping with our nature, so we can be filled with the
fullness of God according to our capacity.

The passage is hardly unknown, but have we begun to assimi-
late it, to realize what it presents as possible? To have, as it were
inside us, God: Father, Son, and Holy Spirit? It is like entering
some oriental tale or dreamworld in which huge mythical creatures descend among the humans. The familiar words, read many

times over, refuse to come into focus, to release what it is they are saying. "Christ lives in me" says Paul, to return to Galatians, and while believing it of him and of ourselves, I imagine we cannot quite get our mind around it. Is that again the point? The words certainly express a personal awareness and a determined choice, but they also state a fact. The Christian only lives because Christ is in him, to change him, to resurrect him, to *give* him life. When Jesus prays for his disciples throughout history that "they all may be one; as thou, Father, art in me, and I in thee, that they also may be one in us" (John 17:21) and declares that he has given them the Father's glory "that they may be one, even as we are one; I in them, and thou in me" (vv. 22–23)—that is, when he speaks of believers as being "in" God and of God as being "in" believers—he is clearly looking to a situation as fact. Perhaps we should live out the fact without probing it or even being very conscious of it. Simone Weil (in the section "Necessity and Obedience" of *Gravity and Grace*) explains the utter surprise of the "righteous" on the Day of Judgment at being told that they have done numerous acts of kindness to Christ: "I was an hungred, and ye gave me meat, etc." (Matthew 25:35–36), acts of which they are entirely unaware, by suggesting that they did what they did "in no way for Christ, they could not prevent themselves from acting so because Christ's compassion was in them." Paul was consumed by the desire to see God glorified, as was Jesus. His desire *was* Jesus in him. If we could make the first three requests in the Lord's Prayer our overriding obsession, maybe that would suffice—if we *wanted* above all that on earth as in heaven God's name be hallowed, his kingdom come, his will be done.

Coleridge had written similarly in *Aids to Reflection.* In the "Corollaries" to the fifteenth of the "Moral and Religious Aphorisms," he argues that motives "are symptoms of weakness, and supplements for the deficient Energy of the living Principle, the

Law within us." Put another way, they are the result of the Fall, the loss of a natural, creaturely harmony with the will of the Creator. The New Testament speaks freely of the liberty of the Christian: "ye have been called unto liberty" (Galatians 5:13); "where the Spirit of the Lord is, there is liberty" (2 Corinthians 3:17); "the truth shall make you free. . . . If the Son therefore shall make you free, ye shall be free indeed" (John 8:32, 36), which liberty is offered by the Scriptures. To read them, says James in an interesting phrase, is to look into "the perfect law of liberty" (James 1:25). If we could say, "I no longer live, but Christ lives in me," we would know the perfect freedom of spontaneous obedience, because we would not be acting from this or that motive, for this or that reason: Christ would be "the living Principle, the Law within us," and we would not be able to prevent ourselves from, say, giving food to someone who was hungry. Jesus's yoke would be easy indeed.

This is, however, a counsel of perfection, an ideal made distant by the persistence of sin. It is sin that means that we cannot be always unconsciously obedient, that we can only on occasion have our left hand ignorant of what our right hand does. Coleridge, who writes in the same "Corollaries," "There is a sweet and holy blindness in Christian Love, even as there is a blindness of Life, yea and of Genius too, in the moment of productive Energy," also writes: "The more *consciousness* in our Thoughts and Words, and the less in our Impulses and general Actions, the better and more healthful the state both of head and heart." (*Impulse* is also, curiously, Simone Weil's word in the same context.) We need to be conscious in our thoughts of what is implied in the words "Christ lives in me"; we have to make the effort to understand, in our experience, what it means to have Christ living his life in our life. Meditating hard on his quite extraordinary, alien-intimate presence can help to make that presence more real. We must certainly learn to see others, the phenomenal world, ourselves, with Christ's eyes, to think with his mind, to feel with his heart. We should act as he acts, speak as he speaks, be as he is, this *as* being quite different from the *like* of imitation, from endeavoring to be like Jesus seen merely as the supreme moral example. From time to time, when observing joyfully some natural phenomenon, which may be nothing more momentous than a small squirrel foraging in the lawn, I have the sudden impression that it is Jesus rejoicing. Seeing my wife, I sense that it is Jesus loving her. I also remember yet again, however, T. S. Eliot, praying at the end of *Ash-Wednesday* not to be mocked with falsehood.

We need a reorienting of our vision—we need *vision:* to see unbelievers as dead, Christians as dead, everything as new, living as Christ, Christ living in us. We shall not be able fully to understand. As Coleridge also writes, commenting on the sixth Aphorism, the aids of the Spirit are beyond our awareness, as are the first movements of our own will. Or, as he puts it more tellingly: "The chameleon darkens in the shade of him who bends over it to ascertain its colors." Without seeing clearly in the deeps through which I have been swimming, for Christians to heed them intently and live in their light would surely make a world of difference and a different world.

3

Heaven Is Here

Where God is, there heaven is.

—Teresa of Ávila, *The Interior Castle*

I

"REPENT: FOR THE KINGDOM of heaven is at hand." This is how Jesus begins his preaching, in the Gospel of Matthew (4:17) and in that of Mark (1:15), who uses the term "kingdom of God." John the Baptist's message had been the same: "Repent ye: for the kingdom of heaven is at hand" (Matthew 3:2), as will be that of the twelve disciples. Sending them to "the lost sheep of the house of Israel," Jesus commands them to preach: "The kingdom of heaven is at hand" (Matthew 10:6–7). He later instructs the seventy to announce that "the kingdom of heaven is come nigh unto you" (Luke 10:9) and to rebuke any who refuse them with the same words: "be sure of this, that the kingdom of God is come nigh unto you" (v. 11). The word for "is at hand" or "is come nigh" being on each occasion *ēvgiken,* Matthew, Mark, and Luke clearly insist (or the Spirit insists through them) on the closing-in of another world.

The immediate meaning would be that Jesus's incarnation itself brings the kingdom of heaven near to humans, and that the as yet revealed-and-concealed crucifixion and resurrection will shortly climax God's revelation of himself and of the demands he makes. Now is—or then was—the accepted time for the Jewish people (in the first instance) to learn anew and to commit themselves to the Messiah. Hence in John the Baptist the sense of wonder and urgency and in the Evangelists the awareness of the moment, of the momentous. Yet Jesus also informs the disciples that "this gospel of the kingdom shall be preached in all the world (until) the end" (Matthew 24:4). Even after the unique and critical epoch of Jesus's work on the earth, the kingdom of heaven, or of God, is the focus of preaching, and this kingdom is always at hand, is always about to be here. Yet Jesus tells the Pharisees, "if I cast out devils by the Spirit of God, then the kingdom of God is come unto you" (Matthew 12:28; see also Luke 11:20), and when they ask him on another occasion at what time the kingdom of God *will* come, he replies: "the kingdom of God is among you" (Luke 17:21; "is within you" in the King James Version seems inaccurate).

The reader is told both that heaven is at hand and that heaven is here. And Jesus goes further in this latter direction. In telling Nicodemus that "except a man be born of water and of the Spirit, he cannot enter into the kingdom of God" (John 3:5), he clearly implies that whoever believes and is baptized (Mark 16:16) *enters* into the kingdom, here and now—that, for him at least, the kingdom is decidedly here. He declares on another occasion: "The law and the prophets were until John: since that time the kingdom of God is preached, and every man presseth into it" (Luke 16:16). Elsewhere, however, the entering is presented as a future event. Luke describes Paul and Barnabas as exhorting the disciples to "continue in the faith, and that we must through much tribulation enter into the kingdom of God" (Acts 14:22), presumably after death. Jesus had warned his hearers in a similar perspective: "except your righteousness shall exceed the righteousness of the scribes and Pharisees, ye shall in no case enter into the kingdom of heaven" (Matthew 5:20). He had rehearsed for his followers the signs that would precede his return, concluding thus: "when ye see these things come to pass, know ye that the kingdom of God is nigh at hand" (Luke 21:31). He demands in his hearers a sense of urgency, while yet referring to events in the far future and beyond their lifetime. He is speaking to his contemporaries in Palestine and also to all Christians throughout the ages. He declares the kingdom to be near at his Second Coming as he had declared it to be near during his incarnation. Luke's word for *near* is *engus*, recalling the verb used elsewhere for drawing near: *engizō*. As so often in the gospels the present and the distant future seem to merge. The reason is presumably that Jesus and through him the Evangelists see as God sees, all time appearing at once before God's eyes, an event in the future not being something for which he has, as it were, to wait, an event in the past not being something he remembers. Our puzzlement in reading such passages teaches us the limitation of our vision and, here as always, that God's manner of being is infinitely different and incomprehensible. In this particular instance, the mingling of the times suggests that, in a way I shall need to explore, the kingdom of heaven is at once with us and far off—is infinitely near.

I have insisted, by doggedly quoting it, on the importance of the expression "kingdom of heaven" or "of God," in part because it does not seem to figure spontaneously in our thoughts on Christian preaching and on the way any Christian presents his faith. That the kernel of the gospel is the crucifixion and resurrection of Christ does not exclude—indeed, it implies—the kingdom of God. This is clear from the references in the Acts of the Apostles to Philip "preaching the things concerning the kingdom of God, and the name of Jesus Christ" (Acts 8:12) and to Paul "preaching the kingdom of God, and teaching those things which concern the Lord Jesus Christ" (28:31). To proclaim the kingdom of God is to present God as more than the answer to our needs and to our questions—to reveal him as sovereign, as King.

2

In a sense, the question of the actual presence of heaven is answered already. We know that we are not in heaven. If this is heaven, something's amiss. And we should refuse to join any heaven that would have us as members, just as we are. We also know that "no man hath ascended up to heaven" (John 3:13) and that we are in that sense excluded. One statement provided by Paul, almost a counterexample, is clearly exceptional, but also, incidentally, greatly enlightening: "I knew a man in Christ above fourteen years ago . . . such an one caught up to the third heaven. And I knew such a man . . . how that he was caught up into paradise, and heard unspeakable words, which it is not lawful for a man to utter. Of such an one will I glory: yet of myself I will not glory, but in mine infirmities" (2 Corinthians 12:2 5). Commentators assume that Paul is recounting his own experience, while not appearing to do so and thereby avoiding self-advertisement, and they leave the matter there. Yet in referring to himself in the third person, he surely sees the otherness of the self to which the experience occurred. It was Paul and yet not Paul who underwent a translation to heaven, an event no doubt full of wonder but shrouded in unknowing: "whether in the body, I cannot tell; or whether out of the body, I cannot tell" (v. 2). He can boast of "such an one" since he has the impression of praising someone else, a close acquaintance yet indescribably different. The passage would imply that any highly elevated spiritual experience, any touch of the heavenly here and now, occurs to the other, transformed self that one is to become. The passage throws light on an equally mysterious realization of Paul's on which I paused in the previous lecture, that he no longer lives, "but Christ liveth in me" (Galatians 2:20).

Heaven as the kingdom of God is for all of us, including Paul, what we inherit, according to the term he himself uses several times in his letters. He too has to wait, though in full confidence: "the Lord . . . will preserve me unto his heavenly kingdom" (2 Timothy 4:18). God, being God, is always in part hidden, and, in our fallen world, heaven is hidden likewise. What we have is glimpses, those in the New Testament being the clearest and fullest. We are shown Jesus at his baptism sighting the other world: "the heavens were opened unto him, and he saw the Spirit of God descending like a dove, and lighting upon him" (Matthew 3:16; see also Mark 1:10). At the transfiguration a window seems to open on to heaven: the three disciples see Jesus transfigured in a supernatural light and conversing with Moses and Elijah. In Luke's version, the latter appear "in glory" and the disciples *see* this glory of heaven (Luke 9:31–32). Stephen, having addressed the Jews with the same indignation as that of Paul when accusing the Gentiles in the first chapter of Romans, "looked up steadfastly into heaven, and saw the glory of God. . . . And said, Behold I see the heavens opened" (Acts 7:55–56). These famous moments are given us, no doubt, not to show us heaven, but to name its "glory," which is more than radiance and attracts both the imagination and the soul; to show an openable way even more promising than the veil of the temple being "rent in twain"; to create the wonder necessary to draw us from a religion of beliefs and practices to a new life of vision, faith with its works, and hope.

And is not the Bible itself such a glimpse? If, as we say partly through habit, the Bible is God's word, we only need to open our ears and our selves to hear him speaking. The Bible, standing on our shelves, forgotten in the attic, lying around in second-hand bookshops, is itself an opening on to heaven.

We are also given glimpses of heaven in our lives. Certain people, or moments with people—what T. S. Eliot would call "moments in and out of time," which are equally moments both here and elsewhere—surprise by their strangeness, by the hint they include of a world of love and righteousness. Such glimpses are certainly inspired from above. Others come from our own efforts—though we cannot know the interest that God takes in them nor the extent to which his Spirit may be aiding us. I think in particular of the whole range of the arts, and above all of one that is not mine, of music. To listen attentively to music is to apprehend, as I said in the previous lecture, both heaven and one's exclusion, to sense its hereness and magnetic nearness. Music in itself, without words even when words are present, creates unknown emotions and constitutes its own, unnatural order. Why should it have such power to draw us into—to surround us with—a weird and superior world, if not to make us aware of what, if we are Christians, we call heaven and, if we are not, we puzzle to identify?

As if to convince us of the difficulty of grasping heaven, Jesus tells his hearers not what the kingdom of heaven is, but what it is "like," in all three synoptic gospels and in Matthew's in particular, as if Matthew, realizing that this was a constant teaching of Jesus's, wanted to stress, like him, the elusiveness of this central fact in a human world estranged from heaven. If we try to grasp "the kingdom of heaven" we learn that it is like treasure hidden in a field, a net, a householder, a grain of mustard seed. At the same time, however, the parables tell of purely worldly matters, most of them quite ordinary (a man sowing a field, a woman mixing yeast and flour), as if to suggest that the kingdom of heaven, though beyond our reach, is all around us.

Heaven Is Here

For heaven *is*, in a way, curiously here. Look closely, for example, at what is said in the Letter to the Hebrews: "it is impossible for those who ... have tasted of the heavenly gift, and were made partakers of the Holy Ghost, and have tasted the good word of God, and the powers of the world to come, if they shall fall away, to renew them again unto repentance" (Hebrews 6:4–6). The passage is chilling, but it speaks—even with reference to those who have fallen away—of tasting the heavenly gift and of tasting the powers of another world—a world still "to come" since we live in hope. For a while, heaven was present, and this is the comparison that follows: "the earth which drinketh in the rain that cometh oft upon it, and bringeth forth herbs ... receiveth blessing from God: but that which beareth thorns and briers is rejected, and is nigh unto cursing" (vv. 7–8). As so often, the Bible draws one into the familiar and earthly, not so as to render an argument easier to understand, but to reveal the analogy between human life and the life of the creation. Those that fall away produce the acts of a fallen humanity as the earth which bears "thorns and briers" reproduces the "thorns ... and thistles" of a ground "cursed" by God as a consequence of the Fall (Genesis 3:17–18). The two expressions are in fact the same, since the author of Hebrews has transferred into his text the Greek words of the Septuagint translation of the passage in Genesis: *akanthas kai tribolous*. But the poetic and theological beauty of the comparison is in that earth *drinking* the rain that "cometh oft upon it." The fallen-away have tasted, the earth drinks, and it imbibes a rain that comes to it often, as grace comes often and generously to the Christian. The earth that drinks and the Christian who tastes, and more than tastes, sense their being fed from elsewhere and of having that gift within them.

And here is Paul, writing to the Romans: "the kingdom of God is ... righteousness, and peace, and joy in the Holy Ghost" (Romans 14:17). Where righteousness, peace and joy are, there is the kingdom of God. If we know these things, we know the kingdom, and whether we realize it or not, heaven is at work in us. The continuation offers a surprise of a different nature: "For he that in these things serveth Christ is acceptable to God" (v. 18). That acts of righteousness constitute service, and peace in the sense of being a peacemaker, is as one expects: but joy? Paul seems to be teaching that joy, and perhaps peace in the sense of being at peace and receiving Jesus's peace, and maybe the righteousness that one seeks in one's relation to God—that these ways of being are a form of service, a conforming of ourselves to what God wants from us and a realization of heaven here.

Paul goes further in another passage to which I referred briefly in the previous lecture: "your life is hid with Christ in God" (Colossians 3:3). (It is amazing how often such uncanny sayings occur in the Scriptures, until one remembers that the Scriptures come from elsewhere.) Rather than heaven being sensible here, we ourselves seem to be present, in ways I do not pretend to understand—who would?—not only in heaven but "in God." We live our life on earth, yet more deeply, as I think we realize in prayer, on a different plane, in a world transcendent and invisible but both joyfully and disquietingly here.

And what of this passage in another of his letters? "Therefore let no man glory in men. For all things are your's; Whether Paul, or Apollos, or Cephas, or the world, or life, or death, or things present or things to come; all are your's; And ye are Christ's; and Christ *is* God's" (1 Corinthians 3:21–23). One must read the many verses leading to this culmination to experience the force of these words, to sense Paul's wonder, for himself as well as for his readers, before this colossal fact. One can hear him writing, idea by idea, in ever-renewed amazement. "All things are yours": all things are ours, yet we possess nothing. Or rather, this immensity that we do not possess is absolutely more ours than the things we do possess. The rich possess nothing; all things belong to the poor. And if Paul is writing from the perspective of eternity, which can envisage our future death and "things to come," he is also writing for now, urging the Corinthians to know that already himself, and Apollos, and Cephas, the world, life, and "things present" are theirs, that they live and move and *are* in the kingdom. He reinforces and perfects this having that is not in our grasp but is a gift from elsewhere by the turn at the end, by the vertiginous final thought: "And ye are Christ's; and Christ is God's." As so often with Paul, our world opens ever further into boundlessness, and I am sure that the very few translations that render the Greek *de* as *but*—"all things are yours . . . but you are Christ's"—miss the point. Our thinking habits lead us to see an obvious change of tack, and to denote it with an adversative *but*. Yet Paul's logic here is quite different: all things are yours, you possess nothing, and indeed, you are Christ's; your non-possessive having of all things is proved by the fact that you belong to Another, and at the same time your belonging to God is the infinite guarantee of your present having.

Paul seems continually aware that he has a profound *vision* of the Christian faith that he must pass on to believers living more shallowly because their thinking is limited and their imagination dormant.

What he tells the Colossians derives its power not from exuberance but from its immense succinctness: God has delivered us from the power of darkness, "and hath translated us into the kingdom of his dear Son" (Colossians 1:13). We have been transferred from one place to another, or rather we are both where we were, in a world of good and evil awaiting its renewal, and in the kingdom of heaven insofar as it is already here, present, invisible, in and around us. Paul has just prayed for the Colossians that God would strengthen them "with all might, according to his glorious power" (v. 11), or literally: according to the power of his glory. The inconceivable and distant *glory* of God impinges even more clearly on our little world in similar words that Paul addresses to the Thessalonians, exhorting them to walk worthy of God, "who hath called you unto his kingdom and glory" (1 Thessalonians 2:12). To learn that one has been called into (*eis*) the divine glory is somewhat breathtaking, since glory (*doxa*) seems to be something like the unimaginable radiance of God himself, which will touch and transform us after death, even our body being raised "in glory" (1 Corinthians 15:43). (*Doxa* is here contrasted with the dishonor—*atimia*—of the earthly body and could have meant simply *honor,* as it often does. The next verse, however, which contrasts the natural body and the spiritual body, justifies translators in giving the word its maximum, supernatural force.) Christians are to realize that they are somehow *in* God's glory, that this unseen radiance surrounds them. Paul is a visionary writer and at the same time, and in the same movement of his mind, a thinker (and not a philosopher in our sense of the word) sharply attentive to the world that emerges for us from the multifarious and—I use the word positively—far-fetched relations among things. One sees it in another of his explorations of glory: "For God, who commanded the light to shine out of darkness, hath shined in our hearts, to give the light of the knowledge of the glory of God in the face of Jesus Christ" (2 Corinthians 4:6). We have, here and now, knowledge of that glory, in the invisible face of Jesus, the light revealing it being a spiritual light shining within us.

Words of Paul's in Ephesians give the same sense of being in heaven already-though-not-yet: God "hath raised us up . . . and made us sit together in heavenly places in Christ Jesus"

(Ephesians 2:6). However well-known the words, they retain their power to startle. We enter such heavenly places, no doubt, in prayer, and fellowship, and worship, in every act of obedience, but do we take fully the idea of *being* in the heavenlies (*epouraniois*)—according to our present capacity—of heaven reaching down to us? A similar passage in the Letter to the Hebrews expands the idea, or rather, the fact, with an exhilaratingly precise copiousness:

> But ye are come unto mount Sion, and unto the city of the living God, the heavenly Jerusalem, and to an innumerable company of angels, to the general assembly and church of the firstborn, which are written in heaven, and to God the Judge of all, and to the spirits of just men made perfect, and to Jesus the mediator of the new covenant, and to the blood of sprinkling, that speaketh better things than that of Abel. (Hebrews 12:22–24)

The comparison here—as in the passage from 2 Corinthians quoted above on seeing the glory of God in the face not of Moses but of Jesus—is with the Hebrews drawing near to the unendurable Mt Sinai. Christians come to no earthly place, but to the heavenly Jerusalem, as if they were already there. The wonder increases as the horizons widen with the appearance of an "innumerable" company of angels and "the general assembly and church" of the firstborn. The accumulation of spiritual otherness reaches a first climax with the sighting of God, who appears specifically as the "Judge" of all: the writer shows with a single word that this vision is not simply to be contemplated and marveled at but that it serves to encourage just acts under the scrutiny of a just God. The second climax comes with the appearing of Jesus, which again includes the unspoken message that we are in the domain not of aesthetics but of spiritual living through the reference to "the blood of sprinkling," to the cross.

This is not a ravishing sight of heaven reserved for the inspired writer, as in John's Revelation. The author of Hebrews assumes that for any Christian a veil disappears between the physical world and the spiritual, that the latter is here if only, with other eyes, we can see it. The final allusion to Jesus's death suggests that if we die daily and thereby resurrect daily, *this* is what we resurrect to.

4

Another approach to the hereness of heaven is to consider the fact that, having begun by preaching that "the kingdom of heaven is at hand" (Matthew 4:17), Jesus declares, as the first of the Beatitudes: "Blessed *are* the poor in spirit: for their's is the kingdom of heaven" (5:3). The last of the Beatitudes is equally: "Blessed *are* they which are persecuted for righteousness' sake: for their's is the kingdom of heaven" (v. 10). Jesus leads into and out of a series of blessings that may be for now but come with a future tense suggesting their fulfillment after death (they that mourn *shall be* comforted, etc.) by blessings that, while they will certainly be perfected in the afterlife, come with a present tense in Matthew's Greek (*estin*) and are seemingly already enjoyed here. The other blessings could have taken this form—blessed are they that mourn for comfort is theirs, blessed are the meek for the earth as an inheritance is theirs, and so on—but they did not. And as the initial preaching preceded the announcement of the kingdom of heaven by a command to repent, the most difficult exercise for the unbeliever, so the first blessing, and the one central to the gospel, depends on being poor in spirit, perhaps the most difficult attainment for the Christian.

And what of the presence on earth of angels? When the angel of the Lord "appeared" to Moses (Exodus 3:2) or to Gideon (Judges 6:12) or to the future mother of Samson (Judges 13:3), how are we to understand this appearing? The short answer is that we cannot understand because we have not been told. We instinctively assume that the angel came from somewhere else and, as it were, materialized in front of the person concerned. He might equally well have simply made himself visible, however, dwelling in a world foreign to our world of space and time and yet permeating it. True, the angel for Gideon firstly "came" (Judges 6:11)—and, arrestingly and engagingly, "sat under an oak"—and Samson's mother also speaks of the angel as having *come* to her (Judges 13:6). When the angel *comes* a second time (v. 9) she informs her husband thus: he "hath *appeared* unto me, that *came* unto me the other day" (v. 10). Between the two appearances, the husband asks God to allow the angel he has *sent* to "*come* again" (v. 8). The Hebrew corresponds to this shift between appearing and, on the other hand, coming or being sent—a shift particularly remarkable in verse 10—and seems to convey the unsoundable relation between two unequal worlds and the necessary limitation of our minds and language.

In the New Testament, an angel of the Lord "appeared" to Zacharias in the temple (Luke 1:11), and an angel "appeared . . . from heaven" to Jesus after his anguish in the garden (Luke 22:43). In all of these appearances so far the same word (*ōphthē*) is used in the New Testament and in the Septuagint translations from the Old. Another verb, *ephistēmi,* is used when an angel of the Lord "came upon" the shepherds at the birth of Jesus (Luke 2:9), when two angels "stood by" the women at Jesus's sepulchre (Luke 24:4), when the angel of the Lord "came upon" Peter in prison (Acts 12:7), as also when Jesus "stood by" Paul during his trial in Jerusalem (Acts 23:11). The word implies suddenness, and creates an effect akin to that produced when the angel ceases to speak to the shepherds and "suddenly [*exaiphnēs*] there was with the angel a multitude of the heavenly host" (Luke 2:13), or when, the three disciples being already startled by the transfiguration of Jesus, "there appeared [*ōphthē*] unto them Moses and Elias talking with him" (Matthew 17:3), or when, in Mark's version, "suddenly" (*exapina*) the disciples, looking around, "saw no man any more" (Mark 9:8). The other world is suddenly there, and suddenly not there. The angel who speaks with Gideon also seems to vanish: he "departed out of his sight" (Judges 6:21).

Of course one often does have a clear sense that angels come from elsewhere—the angel Gabriel is "sent" to Mary (Luke 1:26)— and that they depart so as to go elsewhere. The angel who speaks to the parents of Samson "ascended" in an altar flame (Judges 13:20), and the angels who appear to the shepherds of the Nativity, as it were out of the blue, went away from them "into heaven" (Luke 2:15). Jesus himself "was received up into heaven" (Mark 16:19), or "carried up into heaven" (Luke 24:51). Such a physical displacement, however, whether or not it occurs in our measurable and directional space, manifests essentially the transcendence of heaven, a "higher" realm than ours. Angels and the Son of God ascend supernaturally, so as to rise to that realm.

And what of the fact that the Bible nowhere gives angels wings? Cherubim and seraphim have wings, but not angels. It is surely the overwhelming iconic tradition, those innumerable representations in art of angels with wings like birds, allied to our presupposition that if angels appear here they must have come from elsewhere, which causes us to see them flying through the air.

The most revealing passages as to the nearness of heaven occur in the Old Testament, the one dramatic, the other comic. A large force of Syrians with horses and chariots surround the city where Elisha is. His servant panics at the sight; Elisha reassures him by affirming that they are defended by an even greater force, and he prays God to open his servant's eyes "that he may see." God does so, and the servant "saw: and, behold, the mountain was full of horses and chariots of fire" (2 Kings 6:17). This has always seemed to me the clearest and simplest showing of the presence of heaven here. The servant, like the vast majority of Christians, cannot see it; Elisha, the exceptional "man of God" who needs to, can.

The other passage concerns one of the two most famous asses in the Bible. I am not sure how one should read the story of Balaam's ass, but the fact that the animal speaks, and very reasonably, seems less important than its ability to see what to Balaam is hidden. The king of the Moabites sends messengers to Balaam entreating him to curse the Israelites. Balaam sets out, "the angel of the Lord" bars his way while remaining invisible (Numbers 22:22), but the ass sees him and reacts by turning aside into a field, crushing Balaam's foot against a wall and finally falling down under him. God eventually "opened the eyes of Balaam, and he saw the angel" (v. 31). Once again, the angel is there—is here—but cannot be seen, until God opens the eyes. If, in a story whose import is perfectly serious, the folktale comedy serves to mock Balaam, it also underlines, by way of a seeming absurdity, a speaking and clairvoyant ass, the difficulty we have in seeing the presence among us of the heavens, our need that God open our eyes, and the fact that it is sin—Balaam is tempted by a re-ward—that prevents us from seeing as Adam saw.

5

The question is not whether heaven is different from where we are, the reply to that being obvious, but rather: how should we live the idea of heaven? As a remote otherwhere, or as a world infinitively near? In special circumstances humans have had glimpses of heaven; most of us have not. But then neither have we heard valleys that "shout for joy" and "sing" (psalm 65:13), nor heard the sun and moon praising God, nor mountains and hills, nor cattle and birds. We are deaf to the continual song of the creation, which we know from Psalm 148 to be a fact; perhaps we are blind, through sin, to the unceasing presence of heaven. According to the "Ode: Intimations of Immortality," Wordsworth discovered on reaching manhood that a "glory" had passed away from the earth (line 18), whereas, in what he took to be a universal experience, "Heaven lies about us in our infancy!" (line 66). Many must indeed recognize themselves in this famous line, even if they also carry in their memories the fact that they lived, as children, in a cruel world of which they were themselves a sign. That sense of an earlier "heaven" is, in any case, a realization of the adult, an effect of memory, and what one experiences is more accurately the loss of Eden, the knowledge of one's exile. Each of us enacts, provided we are thus blessed, the Fall, here and now, the being refused a world of presence and "glory." If we are even more blessed, by becoming Christians, we sense that what "lies about us" here and now is heaven. And not only in Wordsworth's "Fountains, Meadows, Hills, and Groves" (l. 188)—though the earth is indeed alive with heaven's praise—since in any circumstances we may awaken to the presence of God and of his world. We do not need to be told that we are not in heaven; we do need to be told that, in a sense, we are.

Laying aside my book during a seemingly endless autumn afternoon in our Burgundy garden, I became aware of the quiet complexity of the leaves, branches, and twigs of the hazel tree under which I was seated, of the slow avalanche of green in the lawns and in so many other trees conspiring with the blue of the sky, and of the strength of the sun in the darkness of the shadows. By ceasing to think and absorbing what I saw, I felt the scene deepen and become prodigiously itself, more real than usual and with a different kind of reality, and time dispersed through

Heaven Is Here

having no hold. The very notion of *being* gradually changed. Everything I saw and heard simply *was*, at once withdrawn into itself and part of the whole, while I myself was no longer a self-consciousness, was no longer important, but simply the partaker through whom the phenomenon could be observed. The stillness of the moment seemed to admit a kind of eternity, and the presences around me, including an old stone wall, to be touched with infinity. It was the season of the ripening of fruit, the long moment when the natural creation produces what has been preparing since the spring—produces and yields. All was fruition, fulfillment, beauty, joy, and it needed so little for everything to yield, to become what it already is, the kingdom of heaven.

Many people have this experience, or something like it, hence the popular expression when such and such happened, "time stood still." The Christian might be tempted, not only to receive the experience as a grace, a hint of heaven and of the spiritual richness already awaiting one on earth, but to think also that, in such a mood, it would be good to die and pass into the plenitude of heaven, into even greater beauty and joy. I saw this more clearly than at the time when remembering the event in Paris and writing about it from that distance.

The desire to glide painlessly from what is almost heaven here into heaven entire, which seems at such moments about to absorb and transform the scene, is clearly wrong, since it is not up to us to choose our death while quite neglecting what God determines and what he still has to ask of us. The reflection prompts a deeper disquiet. Wishing too often and too much for glimpses of heaven, thinking too hungrily of its continuous proximity, would divert us from our real Christian work and could cause us to forget that we live in hope, that we place our treasure in a heaven only to be revealed in the afterworld. The fulfillment of autumn looks to the winter of death and to the spring of resurrection.

6

What prevents us from being in heaven is, after all, sin. And that brings one back to the first Beatitude: "Blessed are the poor in spirit: for theirs is the kingdom of heaven" (Matthew 5:3). Turning, while enjoying the idea or the sense of heaven, suddenly to the fact of sin is rather like, when reading in Proverbs of the just man walking in his integrity and of a king in judgment scattering away all evil, coming immediately upon this: "Who can say, I have made my heart clean, I am pure from my sin?" (Proverbs 20:9). The writer is aware that beneath integrity and judgment there are sins, and that beneath our sins there is our sinfulness. As Karl Barth says explicitly in *The Word of God and the Word of Man*, the problem is "not the puppet sins with which we torment ourselves, but the sin of Adam in which we are begotten and with which we are born, the sin of which we shall not rid ourselves as long as time shall last."

The kingdom of heaven belongs to those who are aware of this, to the poor in spirit, and the perfect illustration of this spiritual poverty would be the parable of the Pharisee and the publican in Luke, chapter 18. On a first reading the parable seems wholly straightforward. The Pharisee thanks God that he is not like others, greedy, dishonest, adulterous, and certainly not like "this publican" (Luke 18:11). He fasts twice a week and pays tithes on all that he receives. These formalistic practices clearly derive from an inner striving to be holy. Above all, he feels no need of God as savior, since he believes himself justified by his own works. All the publican says is: "God be merciful to me a sinner" (v. 13). He is the one "justified," says Jesus (v. 14), having humbled himself.

The teaching is limpid. But while we are congratulating ourselves on agreeing with it, on thinking how deeply right Jesus is, does he not require us to look again? The parable is spoken to "certain which trusted in themselves that they were righteous, and despised others" (v. 9). In listening to it, we put ourselves, without thinking, in the place of the publican, and, in so doing, we become the Pharisee. We say to ourselves, in effect: "Thanks to God I am not like others, and decidedly not like this Pharisee: I beat my breast and pray for forgiveness." Or, more particularly: "I am not like this Catholic, with his dogmas drawn from 2 Colossians and 3 Peter." Or "I am not like this Protestant, a heretic with no understanding of tradition." Or "I am not like this liberal Christian, who refuses the conservative-evangelical view of the Bible." Our mostly unconscious attitude says basically: "I am with the humble publican, I am proud to say." Through this further, underlying teaching of the parable, Jesus leads us to realize, it seems, that the relation of the publican to God and to himself is anything but easy to attain. The Pharisee needs anonymous others so as to admire his supposed superiority. The publican, already despised by society as a tax-gatherer collaborating with the Roman occupiers, is alone with God and with the one fact about himself that counts before God: his sinfulness. When he thinks of others, he no doubt esteems them better than himself (Philippians 2:3). We compare all the time; to see others as they are is an effort beyond our means. Yet it is only when one no longer dares to compare oneself with another, for fear of the result, that one approaches the humility of the publican. His humility, simple and unmixed, is a work of faith, necessary and without merit, a gift of grace.

If we could say what the publican says, and say it as he says it, we would be indeed poor in spirit, and the kingdom of heaven would be ours. When he leaves the temple justified, he surely walks in the kingdom of heaven.

The fundamental problem is, as I said, *sin*. If humanity were without sin, heaven would he here in all its glory. It is our sin that has made the world what it is—or given the devil the occasion to do so—and that continues to perform this work of corruption. Each one of us contributes his mite; we have no idea of the consequences of each and every sin we commit. It is *we* who are responsible for the state of the world. Such a thought might well convict us, make of us convicts, and render us poor in spirit. It also brings us back to the opening words of this lecture, Jesus's command to "repent," for the kingdom of heaven, the kingship of God, the world of judgment, is at hand. And repentance leads us to the fourth Beatitude: "Blessed *are* they which do hunger and thirst after righteousness: for they shall be filled" (Matthew 5:6). Continuing repentance, unflagging *metanoia*, the turning about of the mind and of one's whole being, only occurs when the need for righteousness—for ourselves to be righteous, to meet the overwhelming righteousness of God and to submit to his will—becomes a painful and helpless hunger and thirst. And the righteousness of God guides us to the fear of God.

7

How can heaven be here in a fallen world if we do not fear God? Yet such fear is both troublesome to understand and impossible by our own means. It would seem from the evidence that we refuse to look it in the face. It implies awe, but not an awe from which we can turn away, not an awe basically rather pleasant and in our control. Less the awe we feel before a towering mountain than what we would feel before an approaching tidal wave or a forest fire threatening to enclose us. It is right to take seriously Isaiah's exhortation to see the Lord of hosts as holy: "let him be your fear, and let him be your dread" (Isaiah 8:13). Your *dread*—a powerful Anglo-Saxon word supported by the Hebrew. And equally Amos's rhetorical questions: "The lion hath roared, who will not fear? the

Lord GOD hath spoken, who can but prophesy?" (Amos 3:8). Our God is a roaring lion. And also the admonition to Christians in the Letter to the Hebrews: let us have grace to "serve God acceptably with reverence and godly fear: for our God is a consuming fire" (Hebrews 12:28–29). We should read all references to fearing God with such verses in mind—on learning that the early churches were multiplied when "walking in the fear of the Lord" (Acts 9:31), for instance, or on being urged along with the Corinthians to perfect holiness "in the fear of God" (2 Corinthians 7:1).

Before a righteous and fearful God the proper response is silence. Old Testament writers are particularly aware of this need to quell all questions, points of view, talk. "Be still, and know that I am God" (Psalm 46:10); "Hold thy peace at the presence of the Lord GOD" (Zephaniah 1:7); "But the LORD is in his holy temple: let all the earth keep silence before him" (Habakkuk 2:20); "Be silent, O all flesh, before the LORD: for he is raised up [he has aroused himself] out of his holy habitation" (Zechariah 2:13). Only if one is silent can one hear God's voice, and the fear of God produces that silence.

To understand the depth of a proper silence and the riches to which it gives access, one should consider certain biblical moments where being reduced to silence by the fear of God is accompanied by the presence of God, by the nearness of heaven. When God promises Abram descendants as innumerable as the stars, all Abram does is believe him (Genesis 15:5–6). Before and after this moment he finds many things to say, but faced by the immensity and apparent impossibility of God's promise—and perhaps awed by the analogous immensity of the night sky that God shows him—what can only be his fear prevents him from speaking. He *holds his peace* in the presence of the Lord God (Zephaniah 1:7). The publican knows the silence of repentance; here is the silence of faith, at the very moment when justification by faith is demonstrated. Job, when confronted by God answering out of a whirlwind or tempest (Job 38:1), certainly knows fear, in hearing and seeing God (42:5), in heaven being far too close for comfort. He is not silent, but everything he says is the confession that, before God as God, he has nothing to say, and he falls silent with the words: "I abhor myself [or perhaps is implied: I loathe my words], and repent in dust and ashes" (42:6). The book of Job enacts on a far more radical level the famous axiom of Wittgenstein: "Whereof one cannot speak, thereof one must be silent."

Before this God-who-is-God, sovereign, righteous, who works his own will, who appears as God and saves us as God, we are far removed from so many of our ways of proclaiming the gospel, one of which presents Christianity as essentially a means to finding a meaning in the world and a purpose for one's life. It is surely a sign of the Fall that God is so often shown as the answer to our problems precisely by Christian groups that are nevertheless the most faithful to the Bible and impressively active in spreading the good news.

It is God who grants salvation, as it is God who grants fear. In the profoundly evangelical passage in Jeremiah where God promises his people a return from the Babylonian captivity, he undertakes to give them "one heart, and one way, that they may fear me for ever," and repeats his pledge: "I will put my fear in their hearts, that they shall not depart from me" (Jeremiah 32:39–40). A genuine fear of God is the gift of God, to be opposed to the kind of practiced reverence that we are capable of producing and that God himself denounces when describing, in Isaiah, a people who draw near to him with their mouth and honor him with their lips: "their fear toward me is taught by the precept of men" (Isaiah 29:13). Such ersatz reverence is no more godly than what unbelievers feel in certain churches or before Stonehenge. God is not elsewhere. He is there at work. He is here before we are.

Another passage, in Proverbs, also startles: "Let not thine heart envy sinners:/But *be thou* in the fear of the LORD all day long" (Proverbs 23:17). All the day long—it sounds impossible and even unreasonable, on a par with a comparable and insistently repetitive exhortation of Paul's going in a different direction: "Rejoice in the Lord alway: and again I say, Rejoice" (Philippians 4:4). Yet both writers assume, seemingly, not an uninterrupted conscious fearing or rejoicing but an underlying state, a fear or a joy so thoroughly instilled in us that they guide all we do and say and are—so that we may avoid, for example, envying sinners or allowing gloom to detract from our devotion. And a fear "of the LORD," a rejoicing "in the Lord," suppose a relationship—not an emotion but a way of being and acting, given and furthered from above.

This reference to Paul reminds one that godly fear is in no way incompatible with what one might at first consider more "positive" currents in Christian living (love, joy, peace, and so on), and that it coexists in particular with joy—the gospel being *good* news and, as Pound said of literature, news that stays news. One should read this exclamation in Tyndale's *A Pathway into Holy Scripture* (1531) with the fear of God in mind: "*Evangelion* (that we call the gospel) signifieth good, merry, glad and joyful tidings, that maketh a man's heart glad, and maketh him sing, dance and leap for joy . . . he cannot but be glad, and laugh . . . if he believe that the tidings are true." The rush of synonyms and the cascade of repetitions, which express more truly than would a nice economy of terms the unspeakable exuberance of joy in being a Christian, take on a further depth if one realizes that this gladness, when fully turned towards the God who gives it, is one of the faces of fear.

The fear of God, which teaches his eternal power and Godhead, his incomprehensible otherness, also discovers his nearness. A psalm expresses concretely the mysterious fact: "The angel of the LORD encampeth round about them that fear him,/And delivereth them" (Psalm 34:7). The passage in 2 Kings 6, which recounts the opening of the eyes of Elisha's servant so that he can see the horses and chariots of fire, speaks of a heavenly militia present on a particular occasion. The psalmist reveals that this presence is, as it were, normal for all those who fear God, at any time and in any place. Heaven is here when one fears God. No doubt the more one fears him, the closer he is.

"Where God is, there heaven is": if we desire God, heaven will be here as well. I believe the Lord's Prayer shows us the way to this heavenly presence. If we pray firstly for God, for the prosperity of his name, kingdom and will, the reason is certainly that we must be led out of ourselves and shown that our great and primary concern in life is God. Doesn't this also teach that when we pray for ourselves, this too is for God's sake? We are to resist temptation, for example, so as of course to advance our salvation by refusing a sin, but essentially so as not to offend God. "Against thee, thee only, have I sinned," says the psalmist, "and done this evil in thy sight" (Psalm 51:4). Efforts to be holy equally belong to our salvation, but they too have God as their focus: "Be ye holy," says God, "*for I am holy*" (1 Peter 1:16, quoting the repeated injunction in Leviticus 11:44, 45; 19:2; 20:26). And if the prayer of prayers begins in heaven ("Our Father which art in heaven," Matthew 6:9; Luke 11:2) and descends towards us, doesn't Jesus also guide us to understand that by progressively ascending towards God, by following the petitions from last to first and by their being answered in our lives, we would be fully with God and thoroughly in heaven? We ask lastly to be delivered from evil, or from the evil one. If this were accomplished, we would satisfy the previous petition by not entering into temptation. Our sins or debts would then be forgiven, and we would be able perfectly to forgive all who are indebted to us. Forgiven and forgiving, we would be capable of receiving our daily bread, of hearing every word that proceeds from God and feeding on the bread of life. If that were so, we would do the will of God with such unhesitating alacrity that it would be done in earth exactly as in heaven, and God's kingdom would therefore have come. That being so, his name would be hallowed, and we would find ourselves with our Father, in heaven.

In this inexhaustible prayer, the hinge is surely the petition much better translated: "Thy will be done, as in heaven, so on earth"—as in the Greek, and as way back in the Vulgate and in the Gothic Bible of Ulfilas: *swe in himina jah ana airþai.* The descent to earth, picked up in the Greek by the next word, *bread,* teaches that the will of God is central, on earth as in heaven, and that when God's will is obeyed flawlessly, there is heaven. Doing God's will, even unconsciously, brings heaven here.

As we sometimes think we shall go elsewhere after death, so we think heaven is definitively elsewhere when alive. But if we obey, even with our present, defective deference, the world about us opens and deepens, trembling with the breath of heaven.

4

Seeing Revelation

THE WRITING

> I turned to see the voice that spake with me.
>
> —Revelation 1:12

I

IN MY END IS MY BEGINNING. As I announced at the start, this book results not from my having certain important things to say but from my seeing a number of important matters in the Bible that asked to be explored; and not from any kind of expertise but, on the contrary, from the acknowledgement of my lack of understanding. Revelation, the climactic summation and finale of the Bible, is also the work that most decisively confronts and proves that incomprehension. And which, at the end of the struggle, finds me happy to be left wondering, in both senses of that deep-searching word.

I proceed by asking questions. Anyone reading the many interpretations of Revelation, often brilliant and coherent though only temporarily persuasive, might ask *why* the work is difficult, *why* it should give rise to such conflicting readings. If the revelation was sent to John, according to the opening verse, so that he relay it to his readers for their instruction, why do we find ourselves arguing about what it states and remaining puzzled? No doubt as much could be said of the rest of the Bible. In the devil's grim comedy, Christians throughout the ages, fighting over interpretations, have played the role of adversaries to one another and accusers of the brethren. But at least we know that errors, approximations, and dissensions come from our fallen condition, whereas Revelation seems deliberately to perplex us. Since I suppose (as Ransom says in C. S. Lewis's *Perelandra*, much to the amusement of an unfallen Eve) that God knows what he is doing, our perplexity must be necessary and for our good. Perhaps it also shows us that what is actually said in the work is what counts, and the way it is said: a kaleidoscope of images that implies another kind of reading from that to which our Western culture has accustomed us.

In asking questions of the manner in which the vision in Revelation moves forward by a series of repetitions and transformations, one also discovers from a new perspective that heaven is here and yet not, and that fear is a factor in that nearness and distance.

The questions will be in part those of a poet and those of a Christian responding to the injunction, in only the third verse of the prophesy, to heed "those things which are written therein."

2

The first question is: how did John write Revelation? The short answer, of course, is that we cannot know. We are out of our depth, not being writers of Scripture and, above all, never having had the experience of God-given visions. What we are told is that John sees and hears. In his first letter the same apostle marvels that he has known in the flesh the Son of God, the Word of life: "That which was from the beginning, which we have heard, which we have seen with our eyes, which we have looked upon. . . . For the life was manifested, and we have seen it. . . . That which we have seen and heard declare we unto you" (I John I:I-3). In Revelation he is equally insistent: what he declares is what he has seen. "I saw seven golden candlesticks; and. . . . one like unto the Son of man" (I:I2-I3), "I looked, and, behold, a door" (4:1), "I saw . . . a book" (5:1), "I saw a strong angel" (5:2), "I beheld, and, lo . . . a Lamb" (5:6), and so on through to the final chapter: "I John saw these things, and heard them" (22:8). In all three of his letters, his having seen and heard Jesus guarantees the truth of what he writes. In Revelation, the unceasing succession of lookings and seeings alerts the reader, as in Old Testament prophecy, not only to the eyewitness credentials of the writer but even more to the nature of what he has to say. I shall return to this; I note for the moment the obvious fact, that no reading of the work may ignore this emphasizing of things seen.

He similarly stresses hearing. The revelation even begins there—"I was in the Spirit . . . and heard . . . a great voice" (1:10)—and it continues in the same vein: "the first voice which I heard was as a trumpet talking" (4:1); "I heard the voice of many angels" (5:11); and "I heard . . . one of the beasts saying, Come and see" (6:1). The series of voices culminates when John, having seen a new heaven and a new earth and the holy city coming down from God, declares: "And I heard a great voice out of heaven (better: from the throne) saying, Behold, the tabernacle of God is with man" (21:3). A poet may respond in his own way to "voices" that he hears, and that come, on each occasion, with matters asking to be explored. He certainly doesn't catch the voice of an angel or any other voice from heaven. Expressions, fragments of language, single words unthought of a moment before, sound to his inner ear and constitute, at his merely human level, a part of what he can know of inspiration. John is still a writer when he finds himself becoming a seer: he listens and hears on an eminently higher plain. It seems obvious that Revelation is a witness to what he has heard, yet one easily forgets this when analyzing his elaborate theology.

And why does the first voice that he hears, and that ushers in the whole visionary and auditory experience, sound from behind him?—"I was in the Spirit on the Lord's day, and heard behind me a great voice" (1:10). A poet can at least half understand this inception of a work to be undertaken, which in his case may be a word, or phrase, or the memory of something said, which, sounding suddenly in his mind and arriving out of the blue and, as it were, from behind, from the part of himself that is unseen and hidden, promises and demands a poem to receive it. John continues: "And I turned to see the voice that spake with me. And being turned, I saw seven golden candlesticks" (1:12). The stress on turning ("I turned. . . . And being turned") underlines the otherness of the world into which John is about to enter, an otherness which exegesis may not diminish. The verb used, *epistrephō,* denotes elsewhere in the New Testament the act of being converted, as in Peter's sermon at Pentecost: "Repent ye therefore, and be converted" (Acts 3:19). Small details loom large to suggest the newness and the utter strangeness of what John will undergo, and with him the reader, and the need for both to change direction so as to see.

At the same time it is John and not someone else who is chosen to pass on the revelation—John with his own history and his own reading of the Old Testament and his own life of reflecting on the Christian promise. One may assume, after much thought, that all the biblical writers are inspired by the Holy Spirit through their thinking and feeling, and that, while being inspired, they are mostly conscious of trying to understand and of searching for the words that will accomplish their understanding. David reflects in anguish on what he has done to Bathsheba and Uriah, and when he thinks down to the root definition of his fault: "Against thee, thee only, have I sinned" (Psalm 51:4), the thought is both his own and a gift from the God he has offended. Paul's similarly unfathomable awareness that it is not he who lives but Christ who lives in him (Galatians 2:20), comes from both his own awareness of the mystery of his self and from the Spirit guiding him to that awareness. With John, however, as with the Old Testament prophets, the intervention of the Spirit is abrupt and quite clear. John receives visions from elsewhere, and yet is continuously thinking, and remembering numerous passages in the Old Testament. The fascinating question for the reader, if he chooses to ask it, is how the vivid appearances relate to the complex thinking that they seem to imply.

For John makes clear from the opening verse that he will deliver what he has received rather than present his own views. The well-known words brook no argument: "The Revelation of Jesus Christ, which God gave unto him, to show unto his servants things which must shortly come to pass: and he sent and signified it by his angel unto his servant John" (Revelation 1:1). The route by which the revelation reaches its final addressees is both long and precise: from God to Jesus, to an angel, to John, to God's servants. That the Bible offers us *revelation* is declared most perfectly in what was to become its final book. John's Greek makes the point even more decisively, for the sentence continues: "[John] who bare record (*emartyrēse*) of the word of God, and of the testimony (*martyrian*) of Jesus Christ." Those translations which move from "testified" to "testimony" (one could also imagine "witnessed" and "witness") best show the undeviating path of the truth revealed. By the cognate accusative involved in testifying a testimony (as in living a good life or seeing the sights) the action merges with its object.

We can know nothing about God, creation, salvation, the Christian life, life after death, other than through revelation. As Paul the imposing intellectual writes: "the things of God knoweth no man, but the Spirit of God" (1 Corinthians 2:11). The Spirit reveals what we need and what we can understand, and sometimes more than we can cope with, presumably to humble us by also revealing our limits. Christianity teaches a way of looking that is not ours and that could never have emerged from human thought. Does this account for a curious passage in chapter 7? John sees a great multitude clothed in white and hears them acclaiming the Lamb of God. When one of the elders asks him who they are and whence they come, he can only reply: "Sir, thou knowest" (7:14); the elder goes on to explain. This is the only such moment, yet it suffices to make apparent human ignorance, and the willingness of God to supply the facts.

3

And John's transmission of revelation received, far from being straightforward, poses a challenge to our understanding. He seems neither a passive seer simply relating his visions, nor, on the contrary, a thinker excitedly piecing together, into a new, complex and definitive whole, an amazing array of Old Testament prophecies. The first would be hard to reconcile with the intricacy with which the scriptural texts inform the sights he sees. In chapter 14, and in quick succession, an angel cries "Babylon is fallen, is fallen" (14:8), another angel threatens the worshippers of the beast with drinking "the wine of the wrath of God" (v. 10), another cries "Thrust in thy sickle, and reap . . .

for the harvest of the earth is ripe" (v. 15), and John himself sees the "winepress" of the wrath of God being "trodden" and exuding "blood" (vv. 19–20). The sights and sounds correspond, in order, to Isaiah 21:9, Job 21:20, Joel 3:13, and Isaiah 63:3. One might conclude that the Holy Spirit, having drawn together for this supreme vision numerous prophecies and images that he has already distributed severally in the Old Testament, delivers them, thus assembled, to John. And in fact I can see no constraining reason for denying such a possibility. It would, however, run counter to one's clear sense elsewhere in the Bible that divine inspiration makes use of, and passes through, human character, thought, and talent.

The second view, that John, as a great theologian, is scrutinizing book after book of the Old Testament, any texts of the New that he has available, and perhaps other documents and traditions and is brilliantly constructing, as it were in his study, a masterly treatise—such a view, as far as I know, is nowhere held explicitly. Commentators do not dispute the idea that John had, in one way or another, a visionary experience. Yet the exegeses that discover in the work the most refined patterns suppose a process of strenuous thinking and painstaking construction that in effect denies that John undergoes the experience that he recounts. Does he, or does he not, see what he claims to see?

One needs to consider further John's composition of the work, not to discover exactly how it was conducted, since that is beyond us, but to avoid the insidious error of evacuating the event on Patmos of all reality. John certainly writes, on several occasions, in his own name, though under inspiration. In the opening verse he is prompted to add, to what he has learned concerning the transmission of the revelation, the fact that it was first given to Jesus by God. In addressing the seven churches (1:4–7), he writes in the manner of all the letters of the New Testament. He gives the

The Writing

place and the time of his revelation (1:9–10), like a prophet of the Old. So far, all is written outside of vision and after the event. At the close of the work he speaks in the name of all the "servants" of God (1:1) in responding to Jesus's promise to "come quickly" by the words: "Amen. Even so, come, Lord Jesus" (22:20). He often seems to intervene with comments of his own, in passages where one cannot decide with certainty whether he was led to these thoughts during his vision, or whether he forms them later, when he recounts it. At the close of the vision, for example, an angel carries him in the Spirit to a high mountain from which he sees the new Jerusalem descending from heaven. Having described the city at length, he calls upon Zechariah 14:7, Joel 3:37, and several verses of Isaiah 60 so as to declare that nations and kings shall enter it, that there shall be no night there and that nothing unclean shall be admitted (21:24–27). One can imagine him either remembering the prophecies at the time or searching for the relevant passages at the moment of writing. When he first sees Jesus, "clothed with a garment down to the foot, and girt about the paps with a golden girdle . . . his head and his hairs . . . white like wool, as white as snow; and his eyes . . . as a flame of fire" (1:13), he either at once recognizes in him the visions of Daniel 7:9 and 10:5–6, or he realizes that relationship when beginning his narrative and quotes accordingly.

Aside from the moments where he adds his own reflections, and viewing his experience as a whole, one can envisage a number of creative processes. It could be that John, meditating at depth on the cross and the resurrection, on the continuing war between good and evil (to simplify), on the relation of heaven to earth, on the promise of a new world and on many Old Testament passages that adumbrate the present and the future—that he begins to see new possibilities, with images forming in his mind, and that he finds himself raised by the Spirit to a visionary state in which his meditation is transformed into a series of supernatural events. God would be using John's thought and memory and imagination and guiding him to the truth. The visions would be at once John's and gifts from the God who inspires him. In considering, for example, the twelve tribes of Israel and the twelve apostles and combining them in the unity of the old and the new covenants, John could well see them as twenty-four elders seated on twenty-four thrones around the throne of God and continually worshipping him (4:4, 10). His imagination would lead him to *see* the truth in a way that reason could not discover and as God projects it for him. Similarly, from pondering the imaginative ear of the psalmists, who hear the mountains and hills skip for joy (Psalm 114:4, 6), the pastures and valleys shout and sing (Psalm 65:13) and the heavens declare the glory of God (Psalm 19:1), and in remembering also the four living creatures in the opening chapter of Ezekiel, he could well imagine the whole creation—humans, domestic animals, wild animals, birds—as represented by four supernatural creatures giving glory and honor and thanks to God, day and night, and ceaselessly repeating the "Holy, holy, holy" of the seraphim in the sixth chapter of Isaiah (4:8–9). Here, too, John's reflections and the vision offered by the voice inviting him to enter heaven and to be shown things to come (4:1) would merge. John could then write his visionary meditation, while being inspired to remember.

Such a reading would at least recognize that the visions of truth are divinely given and that John is also thinking hard and gradually composing a single account of the actuality and the future climax of salvation history. However, a reading that supposed that it was John's own process of reflection that gave rise to his vision would have to explain, above all, the origin of the letters to the seven churches in chapters 2 and 3. They would need to be at one and the same time the messages with which

Jesus charged him and the warnings and commendations that he already felt it necessary to deliver. The explanation is hardly convincing. One could also justify the presence of the letters by the desperate suggestion that those opening chapters were a separate text spliced into the whole. (The suggestion has, of course, been made, for other reasons, cutting up the books of the Bible being the international sport of biblical scholars.)

4

It has also been argued that John wrote his visions as he experienced them. This seems more than unlikely: how, taken by a vision, could one be seeing into heaven or watching horrors occurring on earth and at the same time setting everything down in consecutive prose? Yet one moment in the work does give pause. John hears the voice of seven thunders and is "about to write" what they said (10:4), when he is told not to. Although this is the only such reference in the work, it could just be the single instance necessary to inform us that, contrary to what we should expect, John does indeed, on every other occasion, find the means to transcribe his visions. Or is it rather that, lost in a visionary state that presumably surprised him even more than it puzzles us, he simply thinks of himself as writing, his mind still ringing with Jesus's command to write what he sees (1:11, 19)? He writes, after all, in the past tense, so as to narrate what he saw and heard.

A more plausible though still unconvincing view would suggest that John has a number of distinct visions and that he writes down each in turn. One does discover a number of possible pauses in the work, the most obvious being that between chapters 3 and 4. Having found himself "in the Spirit" (1:10) and having heard the letters to the seven churches spoken by Jesus, he sees, "after this," a door opened in heaven and states: "immediately I was in the spirit" (4:1–2). He has a new vision, of the throne of God, the elders and the four living creatures. Another could occur between the end of the narrative of the seven seals and the appearance of the "woman clothed with the sun," described as "a great wonder (better: sign, *sēmeion*) in heaven" (12:1), and another when John sees a further great "sign" (*sēmeion*): the seven angels with the seven last plagues (15:1). He is also newly "carried . . . away in the Spirit" to be shown the "great whore" of Babylon (17:1, 3), and again (21:10) so as to see "the holy city, new Jerusalem" (21:2).

It may be that the visions and the acts of writing occurred thus, consecutively. Yet the work seems clearly to present itself as a single visionary journey, a single experience of being "in the Spirit" and advancing from one marvel to another, finally emerging so as to obey the command to write. An argument in favor of this view—an argument, not a proof—is that, in the opening of the work, we read at least two things that he has learned from his visions before his narrative of the visions begins. How does he know God to be "[that] which is, and which was, and which is to come" (1:4)? Because he has heard the four living creatures acclaiming as holy the Lord God Almighty, "which was, and is, and is to come" (4:8). If he refers, in this same fourth verse, to "the seven Spirits which are before his throne," he is remembering what Jesus said to the church in Sardis, that they are hearing the words of him "that hath the seven Spirits of God" (3:1). John enjoys, surely, a single revelation, sensing the Old Testament references in his visions because they are already present in the complexity of his thinking, or because in the revelatory flash the Spirit enables him to see as an ensemble multiple references that had not yet come together in his mind. Perhaps, at times (as I suggested above), he only realized the density of reference in what he saw at the moment of writing. Any of these possibilities could have been the case in the cascade of quotations that allow John to see at last, as his vision reaches its consummation in glory, the new world and the new Jerusalem. He sees the "new heaven" and the "new earth" (21:1) of which Isaiah only hears the announcement (Isaiah 65:17; 66:22). He hears a great voice out of heaven declaring: "God shall wipe away all tears from their eyes" (v. 4), as had been prophesied elsewhere in Isaiah (25:8). He hears God making whoever "overcomes," a promise: "I will be his God, and he shall be my son" (v. 7) that he had made to David (2 Samuel 7:14) and to Israel (Jeremiah 31:33). He sees the wall of the new Jerusalem with three gates on each of its four sides bearing the names of the twelve tribes of Israel (vv. 12–13) as the realization of the future city revealed in those terms to Ezekiel (Ezekiel 48:31–34). He is aware that "the city had no need of the sun, neither of the moon, to shine in it: for the glory of God did lighten it" (v. 23), exactly as Isaiah had predicted of Jerusalem (Isaiah 60:19–20), and that "the gates of it shall not be shut at all" (v. 25) as Isaiah had equally stated (Isaiah 60:11). On many of these occasions, what John sees and hears transposes the passages quoted in terms of the new covenant, of the Christian and universal church.

The essential point, when one has labored through these complexities, is that John finds himself "in the Spirit" (1:10), and that, at the moment a door opens in heaven and he is told to "come up" into this daunting otherness, the expression recurs (*egenomēn en pneumati,* 4:2), so as to mark the passage into an even higher revelation and also, no doubt, to remind us that John is in an existential state and a spiritual world that must inevitably unsettle our "normal" view of things. John's Revelation cuts across our ways of thinking by moving through outlandish persons and events, and across our ways of seeing by presenting sights necessarily foreign to our visual reality. Even John's being in the Spirit "on the Lord's day" (1:10) might just have a larger significance than at first sight. The expression (*en tē kyriakē hēmera*) came to mean "on Sunday," and may have no more than that meaning here. It is certainly not to be confused with "the day of the Lord" (*hēmera kyriou*) in 1 Thessalonians 5:2: John is not transported to the Day of Judgment. But is it possible that in writing a single expression, in which "*in* the Spirit" and "*on* the Lord's day" are the same word in the Greek (*en*)—"I was in the Spirit (in) the Lord's day"—he intends to convey that the *day* of his revelation was indeed the Lord's, that he was privileged to see, not exactly as Jesus sees, but with a vision much closer to his?

5

Seeing Revelation

THE IMAGES

I

WHATEVER THE CASE, the time has come to ask a second question: why does Revelation teem with images? Why is John not able to tell us straightforwardly what we need to know? We pass here from John's experience as writer to our experience as readers. Certain images, of course, are easily understood in terms of what they represent; they can be expressed in imageless prose. The Lamb of God, who appears throughout, is clearly Jesus in his role of sacrificial victim, innocent and helpless (and yet victorious). But should the presence of this familiar image lead us to explain in the same way—or attempt to explain—the less perspicuous images that crowd our mental vision as we advance through the work? Such a procedure is implied by the introduction to Revelation in the French *Bible de Jérusalem:* "When he describes a vision, the seer translates into symbols the ideas that God is suggesting. . . . To understand him, one must therefore . . . translate back into ideas the symbols he proposes." His "visions have no value in themselves." Is not this thoroughly misguided? It presupposes that John is unconsciously or willfully delivering "symbols" rather than passing on ideas (one wonders why), and that God himself works with ideas (like a theologian juggling with propositions). It assumes that readers of the Bible are all Western intellectuals in need of concepts, and even that God, made in our image, is mostly at home among ideas. Yet, like so many biblical authors, John writes as a poet, and specifically as a visionary poet in prose, while God's way of approaching him may well suggest that not only are God's thoughts not our thoughts (Isaiah 55:8) but that his way of thinking also differs from ours. If the revelation of the present and the future does not arrive in the form of statements, is this not in part to show the otherness of the heavenly vision?

Modern commentators of the book rightly mock earlier generations bent on decoding its message. They too, however, find themselves turning the images into something else. This is even the case with Austin Farrer, who, in *The Glass of Vision* of 1948, declared searchingly of the Bible in general: "We cannot by-pass the images to seize on imageless truth," and yet, in turning to Revelation a year later, in *A Rebirth of Images,* produced a particularly elaborate deciphering. One could conceive a translation of John's text without a single image, each one having been replaced by an interpretation. And after all, if the images are only there to be interpreted, why not? And if the argument put forward for the presence of images is that they are polysemous and therefore brimful of matter, why not simply list their many "meanings"?

It is certainly true that even several unfamiliar images in Revelation carry a meaning that is easily, and perhaps instantly, discovered. The rider of one of the horses that emerge on the opening of the second seal (6:4) is actually presented as the bringer of war to the earth. But he is still a rider on a red horse wielding a great sword. To explain him is not to dispense with him. It might also be advanced that the New Testament constantly reinterprets events, practices, and places in the Old according to the venerable theory of allegory. Paul sees the Israelites who follow the cloud (Exodus 13:21) and cross the Red Sea (14:22) as being "baptized" into Moses (1 Corinthians 10:2), and he goes on to say of the rock that Moses smote to give people drink (Exodus 17:6): "that Rock was Christ" (v. 4). But these interpretations do not explain the images away; they do not imply that, having extracted their meaning, we have no need of them, for they were real occurrences. The Israelites crossed the Red Sea and Moses smote a rock. The events remain, as do John's images.

Could it be that Jesus teaches us, in the text itself, how to read them? He explains the very first vision: "The seven stars are the angels of the seven churches: and the seven candlesticks . . . are the seven churches" (1:20). This seems clear, but can we conclude that our task is similarly to translate the images that are not explained? Our first attempt does appear to work. The twenty-four elders and the four living creatures of John's second vision (chapter 4) are usually seen as representing respectively, as I mentioned above, the twelve tribes and twelve apostles and the whole of creation. (*Catechism of the Catholic Church* §1138, takes this as read.) But can we say, or does it suffice to say, that the elders *are* tribes and apostles and that the creatures *are* the creation? For in thinking further of Jesus's explanation, one realizes that he still leaves us wondering. In particular, what is the "angel" of a church? And why should he leave us to conclude, rightly or wrongly, that the seven churches situated in Asia Minor stand for all Christian communities everywhere and at all times?

What above all is the status of the verb in the statements, "the . . . stars are (*eisin*)" angels and "the . . . candlesticks . . . are (*eisin*)" churches? Jesus does not say that the stars *mean* angels or that the candlesticks *stand for* churches. This is a way, perhaps, of telling us not to discard the image in favor of an explanation, and to *see* that candlesticks and stars, with their particular ranges of suggestiveness, also *are*. When he declares that *a* is *b* he seems to be teaching (though I am aware of the danger involved in putting words into Jesus's mouth) that both *a* and *b* are ways of seeing, that we must read Revelation with this constantly in mind, and that we should recognize that we have entered a way of seeing and understanding that is not ours. To translate it into our way is entirely to miss the point. For Jesus is also teaching that no explanation, which the work volunteers or which we discover, suffices. So the angel who offers to "tell . . . the mystery" of the beast with seven heads and ten horns (17:7) increases it: "The beast that thou sawest was, and is not; and shall ascend out of the bottomless pit, and go into perdition" (17:8). His explanation needs explaining.

And the explanations that we devise resemble paraphrases—the text says *that*, but what it really means is *this*—in the manner of modern translations of the Bible eager to make it easily understandable. I have already quoted one such paraphrase in another work, but I shall quote it again since it fits so perfectly into my argument. The King James Version of Ecclesiastes 11:1, following closely the Hebrew, runs: "Cast thy bread upon the waters: for thou shalt find it after many days." The Good News Bible reads: "Invest your money in foreign trade, and one of these days you will make a profit." The images of bread and of waters have disappeared behind a grotesque "explanation." The reader can no longer meditate on the images, nor enter into the gesture of casting away.

Revelation also moves by degrees into the strangeness which is perhaps its fundamental "message." John begins in our world, at a particular place, Patmos, and a particular time, the Lord's day. All heavenly revelation in the Bible arrives in the midst of ordinary circumstances, often more detailed than here. Ezekiel states with care that in the fifth day of the fourth month of the thirtieth year, as he was among the captives by the river of Chebar "the heavens were opened, and I saw visions of God" (Ezekiel 1:1). Zephaniah pays similar attention to earthly details in announcing that the word of the Lord came to him, "the son of Cushi, the son of Gedaliah, the son of Amariah, the son of Hizkiah, in the days of Josiah the son of Amon, king of Judah" (Zephaniah 1:1). One remembers the Lord appearing to Abraham "in the plains (or by the oaks) of Mamre (as) he sat in the tent door in the heat of the day" (Genesis 18:1). All such moments stress the ordinary here-and-now on which heaven impinges. John's places him and us in our own way of being and seeing before the transporting into a quite other way.

All the opening of the work contributes to this gradual making-strange, to our finding ourselves more and more out of our depth. It begins, after all, from the third verse, as an apostolic letter, with John's greeting: "John to the seven churches which are in Asia: Grace be unto you . . .," and with a doctrinal development on Jesus Christ, the faithful witness, the first begotten from the dead (v. 5). We could (almost) be reading John's Fourth Epistle. We are then given the circular letter to the seven churches, which follows the same pattern though with Jesus as author, and even after the sudden change of worlds when a door in heaven is opened and John passes through it, we are helped on our way, in chapter 5, by the "familiar" vision of angels and created things worshipping God and the Lamb of God, in five brief bursts of praise. With the opening of the seals in chapter 6 we begin the long, humbling, exhilarating journey into not knowing where we are, nor even when.

We assume that John's visions are abnormal, and comfort ourselves by rewriting them according to our "normality," whereas they are moments when reality is revealed, when we see things closer to what they are. The work invites us to probe the idea in several ways. There is firstly the word *like*, which occurs ceaselessly, in its several Greek forms (*hōs, hōsei, homoios*), and which one can easily miss due to its familiarity from daily use, but which carries a powerful charge of meaning. As soon as John is "in the Spirit" he finds himself needing to say that the voice he heard was "as a trumpet" (1:10), and, most remarkably, he can only see Jesus through a series of similitudes. His first glimpse is of one "like the Son of Man" (1:13). Jesus's head and hairs are "white like wool" and "as snow," his eyes "as a flame of fire," his feet "like unto fine brass, as . . . burned in a furnace," his voice "as the sound of many waters," his "countenance as the sun shineth in his strength" (1:14–16). John multiplies the words for *like/ as* in the attempt to grasp what he is seeing. For he is looking at Jesus but seeing him quite differently from when he knew him on earth. The Jesus who has ascended into heaven can only be visualized by comparisons that show, not what he is, but what he is like. Jesus seems to underline this by saying of himself, in the letter to the church of Thyatira, that the Son of God "hath his eyes like unto a flame of fire, and his feet like fine brass" (2:18). When heaven is opened towards the end of the vision, John again sees Jesus, and again notes that "His eyes were as a flame of fire" (19:11–12). This is not the way Jesus is usually presented from the pulpit and in devotional works. However, since John's book, whatever else it may be, is explicitly, in the opening words, "The Revelation of Jesus Christ," this is an image we should not forget when approaching him.

The Images

John has recourse to the same language when he enters heaven in vision and "in the Spirit" (4:2). He again hears the voice "as a trumpet" (4:1), and what he sees is God on his throne, "to look upon like a jasper and a sardine stone," around the throne a rainbow "in sight like unto an emerald" (v. 3), and before the throne "a sea of glass like unto crystal" (v. 6). In the midst of the throne and round about it are the four living creatures, the first "like a lion," the second "like a calf," the fourth "like a flying eagle" (v. 7). Here John uses for each *like* the same word (*homoios*), as if to stress, maybe, this solely available way of seeing and describing. For "like" presents itself as the link between our world and heaven. It continues to do so in John's first apocalyptic vision in the narrow sense of the word. At the opening of the sixth seal "the sun became black as sackcloth of hair, and the moon became as blood; and the stars . . . fell . . . as a fig tree casteth her untimely figs. . . . And the heaven departed as a scroll when it is rolled together" (6:12–14). It continues, in a cascade of occurrences, in John's first vision of nightmare monsters. From the bottomless pit emerge locusts to whom was given "power, as . . . scorpions . . . have power" (9:3) and who were sent to torment the ungodly with a "torment as the torment of a scorpion" (v. 5). Their shapes were "like unto horses prepared unto battle"; their heads bore "as it were crowns like gold"; their faces were "as the faces of men," their hair "as the hair of women," their teeth "as the teeth of lions"; their breastplates were "as it were breastplates of iron"; their wings gave a sound "as the sound of chariots of many horses"; and their tails were "like unto scorpions" (vv. 7–10). And so on through the work, until his vision of the new Jerusalem, "prepared as a bride" (21:3), its light "like unto a stone most precious, even like a jasper stone" (v. 11), being a city of "pure gold, like unto clear glass" (v. 18), with its streets also of "pure gold, as it were transparent glass" (v. 21), and until his vision of the river of the water of life, "clear as crystal" (22:1).

I have set down this characteristic of the work with detailed insistence so as to demonstrate it clearly, since it matters. To say, taking another example, that the beast rising from the sea was "like a leopard" (13:2) is also to infer that it was *not* a leopard; all these instances of *like* tell us equally what the things that John saw were not. In revealing what was shown to him he shows us what we cannot see. *Like* is a fragile link. Since God created us in his "image" and "likeness" (Genesis 1:26)—the perfect sign that *like* implies *unlike*—we are ourselves likenesses, figures of God, comparisons. (One might even say that, as creations of the Word of God, we are figures of speech.) Our creaturely status seems to indicate that, looking in the other direction, we can only envisage God and everything heavenly through the medium of likeness. Already on earth, when the Jesus with whom the disciples have companioned is transfigured, his face shines "as the sun" and his raiment becomes white "as the light" (Matthew 17:2), or "as snow" (Mark 9:3). These many instances of likeness would be the hint that whatever is revealed in Revelation is a likeness, even when no comparison is involved. John sees an image which is like that of a woman clothed with the sun, or which is like a dragon (12:1, 3). And it is John who declares, in his first letter, the consummation of likeness in a likeness without distance, with no sense of reaching-for without attaining: "Beloved . . . it doth not yet appear what we shall be: but we know that, when he shall appear, we shall be like him; for we shall see him as he is" (1 John 3:2).

Like is for the present the limit of our world. Beyond John's likenesses in Revelation lies always something more.

3

A second way of exploring John's revelation of reality is to consider a composite image. The four living creatures ("beasts" in the King James Version), which appear firstly in chapter 4 and which seem to be a vision of the whole creation continually praising God, recall the four living creatures in the opening chapter of Ezekiel, who in chapter 10 identifies them as cherubim. However, there are differences. In Revelation, the creatures have six wings (4:8) and recall the seraphim who appear to Isaiah (6:2). For Ezekiel, they have four wings (1:6), though John's eyes may have been guided by his memory of the Septuagint translation, where Ezekiel, after noting four wings, adds that the feet also were winged, *pterōtoi* (1:7). In Revelation, the first creature resembles a lion, the second a calf or ox, the third has the face of a man, the fourth is like an eagle (4:7). For Ezekiel, each creature has four faces (1:6), and each has the face of a man, a lion, an ox, and an eagle (1:10). When he sees them again, as cherubim, he sees the faces, in order, as those of a cherub, a man, a lion, an eagle (10:14). Why these discrepancies? Why do Ezekiel and John see differently? Had John wished to make his vision conform to Ezekiel's—had he foreseen the fun that certain commentators have in indicating contradictions in the Scriptures—he would surely have done so. Should we not conclude that each of the prophets is shown what he needs to see, and that each sees as best he can. They have partial visions of the truth, since they are glimpsing the invisible. The creatures differ each time they are looked at, because their heavenly reality is beyond us. Hence the appearance of the creatures to Ezekiel, as to John, through the medium of likeness. Ezekiel sees "the likeness (Septuagint: *homoiōma*) of four living creatures," each having "the likeness of a man" (1:5), their hooves being "like" those of a calf and sparkling "like the color of burnished brass" (v. 7). He sees the "likeness of their faces" (v. 10), and their overall "likeness" as "like" burning coals of fire and "like" the appearance of lamps (v. 13). Ezekiel, to whom "the heavens were opened" and who saw "visions of God" (1:1), is equally incapable of seeing directly. Hence also the fact that the four living creatures, whose "meaning" is not given, remain whatever they are.

A third way to examine John's showing of "the things which are, and the things which shall be" (1:19) is via the signs that he sees. In chapter 11, the seventh angel sounds his trumpet and loud voices in heaven declare: "The kingdoms of this world are become *the kingdoms* of our Lord . . . and he shall reign for ever and ever" (11:15). John witnesses once more the final triumph. Chapter 12 then announces a new beginning, through the vision of a woman "being with child" and "travailing in birth" (12:1–2). She appears, John writes, as "a great wonder in heaven" (v. 1), and the word *sēmeion* can have this meaning. Yet the underlying meaning is surely "sign," as with the dragon, who appears immediately as "another wonder (sign) in heaven" (v. 3), and with the angels of the seven last plagues who are seen equally as "another sign in heaven" (15:1).

How should one read the woman as a sign? Since she bears a child "who was to rule all nations with a rod of iron" (12:5) it is presumably right, and necessary, to think of Mary, and Israel, and also Eve, whose "seed" (Genesis 3:15) is attacked by the serpent as dragon. Since Jesus says to the angel of the church in Thyatira: "he that overcometh . . . to him will I give power over the nations: and he shall rule them with a rod of iron" (2:26–27), the child seems also to suggest any faithful Christian, and the woman to evoke the church. In thinking like this we are seeing John's text as allegorical prose, comparable in literary terms to, say, Spenser's allegorical poetry in *The Faerie Queen*. We might then remind ourselves that in reading Spenser we do not forget the narrative, or its characters and images, once we have decided the spiritual lessons they are designed to convey. On the contrary, it is the vivid narrative and the great poetry that claim our attention.

The Images

We read *The Faerie Queen,* not a series of explanations making redundant all that Spenser actually wrote. Even in allegorical poetry, where the existence of implicit meanings is made explicit, we find ourselves in a world of imagination, of images, which adds hugely to any discernable meanings, enriches them, and transcends them. The same is true of Revelation, and clearly so in the case of the woman and the dragon, principal characters of the longest episode in the work. The dragon attempts to devour the child, which is snatched up to heaven; the woman flees into the wilderness; the dragon is beaten by Michael and his angels and cast out of heaven onto the earth; he attacks the woman with a flood that the earth swallows; furious at being thwarted, he goes to make war against those of her seed who are Christians. We also seem to be watching the rush of events along with heavenly spectators, whose spokesman interrupts the action (12:10–12) so as to celebrate Michael's victory and to warn the inhabitants of the earth that the devil has come among them.

As sign, the woman participates in the story of a victory already won and of our nevertheless having to accomplish it. And as sign above all she is what John immediately says of her, "a woman clothed with the sun, and the moon under her feet, and upon her head a crown of twelve stars" (v. 1). She is clearly a figure in the sky, as is the dragon, whose tail "drew the third part of the stars of heaven, and did cast them to the earth" (v. 4). But no astrology is involved. She is seen in that beautifully ambiguous space that is at once the material sky and the realm of God, the vastness of the visible and the invisible kingdom onto which it seems that such a vastness must give. The merging of sky and heaven would be present in John's mind as a Jew, as it is present in the Greek word *ouranos* that he writes. Her sky even combines day and night, as if to suggest, by an image, her being situated between our world and the other. God speaks to us in signs more than in concepts, and his sign language is particularly rich. The value of the woman clothed with the sun is not exhausted in the interpretations we bring to her. Having been given her narrative, we should continue to read it.

John's images are complex and difficult because they constitute an intermediate world, short of heaven but beyond our habitual ways of seeing.

4

The final and most revealing approach would be to reflect on the word *mystery, mystērion*. It occurs early, when Jesus refers to the "mystery of the seven stars ... and the seven golden candlesticks" (1:20). As already suggested, he does not simply decipher the stars and the candlesticks, and by using the powerful and finally ungraspable word "mystery" he reveals them as being in a world to which we do not quite have access. This becomes even clearer with the "great whore" sitting on "a scarlet colored beast ... having seven heads and ten horns" (17:1, 3), the name on whose forehead seems to be "mystery, Babylon the great" (v. 5). (The translators who give: "a name—a mystery!—Babylon the great," or "a mysterious name: Babylon the great," have looked without cause for a way of normalizing the Greek syntax.) John and the reader are presented with a striking image that is apparently itself "mystery." John's reaction is, not unnaturally: "I wondered with great admiration," yet the angel asks him: "Wherefore didst thou marvel?" (vv. 6–7). Many translators—and here, even those of the King James Version—deploy shrewd synonyms, whereas by writing: I wondered ... with great wonder ... why do you wonder? (*ethaumasa ... thauma mega ... ethaumasas*), John accentuates the depth of his marveling and the importance of the angel's reaction. (The Vulgate gets it right: *mīratus sum ... admīrātiōne*

The Images

magna... mīrarīs.) The angel offers to explain "the mystery of the woman, and of the beast that carrieth her" (v. 7), yet, as said above, his lengthy elucidation is at most points obscure. His strange question may well figure in the work to show the gulf between human understanding and that of an inhabitant of heaven, and to signal that the angel's intellection, like that of all those who speak to John, is hardly expressible for our intellect.

It might be objected that the other occurrence of the word *mystery* in Revelation gives it the meaning, not of a continuing mysteriousness but of something once hidden which is now revealed. John hears an angel with an open book declare that when the seventh angel sounds his trumpet, "the mystery of God should be finished, as he hath declared to his servants the prophets" (10:7). As soon as the trumpet sounds, voices in heaven do indeed proclaim, as quoted above, that the "kingdoms of this world are become the kingdoms of our Lord, and of his Christ" (11:15). Through his cross and resurrection Jesus already reigns. Paul writes similarly of God's power to establish his readers "according to the revelation of the mystery [*kata apokalypsin mystēriou*], which was kept secret since the world began (better: for long ages), but now is made manifest" (Romans 16:25–26). He writes of "the mystery which hath been hid from ages and from generations, but now is made manifest to his saints" (Colossians 1:26). Yet here he continues by stating that "the riches of the glory of this mystery . . . is Christ in you" (v. 27). Christ *in* Christians, or *among* them, can now be thought and said, but it remains mysterious. And when he tells the Corinthians "Behold, I shew you a mystery," what he reveals is still beyond our reach: "We . . . shall all be changed, in a moment, in the twinkling of an eye, at the last trump" (1 Corinthians 15:51–52). How are we to understand a trumpet sounding at the end of time, and our being changed, our putting on "incorruption" and "immortality" (v. 53)? What he reveals is indeed a mystery, moving and sublime. The same applies to the words of the angel holding an open book. The kingdoms of this world have become the kingdoms of the eternal God, and we can rejoice in the fact. But do we grasp what that means? In particular, would we say, on looking around, that the mystery of God is thereby finished, given worldwide disobedience? The angel speaks truth, but truth as God and the inhabitants of heaven see it. As John's vision proceeds, and immediately in chapter 12, there is "war in heaven" (12:7) and the dragon goes to "make war" (v. 17) on the earth. All is finished, for a heavenly eye, but we on earth continue to see through a glass, darkly. The angel's reference to the "prophets" to whom the mystery has been declared (10:7) alerts us, perhaps, to the fact that the Old Testament prophets only understood in part the revelation they received, and that even those of the New Testament only saw through the luminous obscurity of their own age. The book of Revelation, though penetrating further and newly into the mystery of God, is our Ezekiel.

A similar effect is created by the word *spiritually, pneumatikōs*. John is told by an angel of two "witnesses," who prophesy and are killed by the beast from the bottomless pit, but who, given new life, ascend into heaven. When recounting their death, the angel states, in a rapid density of allusions: "their dead bodies shall lie in the streets of the great city, which spiritually is called Sodom and Egypt, where also [their] Lord was crucified" (11:8). Translators who replace "spiritually" by "symbolically" or "figuratively" are seeking to draw John's unexpected adverb back into the familiar. They thereby lose what seems to be the point. The speed with which one passes from, no doubt, Babylon and/or Jerusalem to Sodom and Egypt and, while one is trying to hold all this together, to the indication that Jesus was crucified there, surely emphasizes that this composite image of the fallen world,

The Images

97

this imaginative, real place, is viewed in a way not available to our mind—spiritually, perhaps by the Spirit.

All the images in John's prophetic vision are at once revelation and mystery. He sees things beyond ideas, and what is revealed is what he sees. Partial interpretations that he hears are precious indications for our intelligence, but they are nevertheless not designed to empty the images of their life. Hence the importance of the moment when, having heard thunders speak, he is told for once not to write what they said (10:4). In a book that presents itself as prophecy and revelation, this single moment suffices, not only to suggest that there are matters that God wills not to be made known (as when the person whom Paul recalls in considering "visions and revelations of the Lord" hears in paradise words that may not be repeated—2 Corinthians 12:1, 4), but also to remind us that in what is revealed throughout the book there is a further element not yet told. The passage occurs, moreover, a few verses only before the same angel announces that the mystery will be finished (10:10), which finishing remains mysterious.

Reading the work is like watching a film, full of movement, of characters, of abrupt changes of scene, and even more like dreaming and seeing the discontinuous passage of surreal creatures and happenings, with voices constantly intervening. The dream is often a nightmare. We are at once in a dystopia of horrendous beasts, a bottomless pit, and a lake of fire—and in a utopia of God, of the Lamb, of the blessed around the throne, of the new Jerusalem, the new heavens and the new earth. In a magnified, clairvoyant view of the world we know.

6

Seeing Revelation

THE TIMING

I

WHICH PROMPTS MY THIRD QUESTION: when are the events recorded supposed to happen? The very first sentence is quietly amazing, since it tells of things "which must shortly [*en tachei*] come to pass." The third verse insists: those who read or hear the prophecy are warned to heed it, "for the time is at hand [*engys*]." Yet we go on to read of the opening of a book of seven seals, of the sun becoming black, of monsters and plagues, of the descent of the heavenly Jerusalem. On reaching the end of the work we are told that what we have read is true, and that it shows us "the things which must shortly [*en tachei*] be done" (22:6). John is again ordered to reveal what he has seen, "for the time is at hand [*engys*]" (22:10). Jesus assures us, no fewer than three times: "I come quickly [*tachy*]" (22:7, 12, 20). The insistent confirmation of what was said at the beginning reinforces our puzzlement; Jesus has been coming shortly for two thousand years.

The way to understanding, within our limits, passes through the expression, "the time is at hand" (1:3; 22:10). The word for time is *kairos*, which indicates a fixed time, but also the opportune time, the proper time. The right time, for choosing the will of God, is always near, just as the kingdom of heaven is always close. John surely re-echoes the sense in the Old Testament prophets of the urgent proximity of God and of his acts. Isaiah hears God say: "My righteousness is near; my salvation is gone forth, and mine arms shall judge the people [better: the peoples]" (Isaiah 51:5; "near" in the Septuagint is *engys*). Ezekiel (30:3), Joel (3:14), Obadiah (v. 15) and Zephaniah (1:7, 14) all proclaim that "the day of the LORD is near" or "at hand" (the Septuagint giving *engys* on each occasion). By gathering ancient revelations of the nearness of what is distant, in God and in time, John shows the continuing strangeness of time as created by God and the need to learn that strangeness, in part by studying how to read his prophecy. Paul has the same sense of the impending of what we call the future. "The Lord *is* at hand [*engys*]," he tells the Philippians (4:5), when thinking of the Lord's return. To the Romans he writes: "[Do this], knowing the time [*kairon*], that now *it is* high time to awake out of sleep: for now *is* our salvation nearer [*engyteron*] than when we believed. The night is far spent, the day is at hand [*ēngiken*]" (Romans 13:11–12).

Revelation snatches us, from the fifth chapter to the last, into the workings of an alien time. Already in chapter 10, an angel swears that "there shall be no more delay" (10:6, a translation preferable to that of the King James Version), yet events continue to multiply, and when we look up from the book on finishing it, the customary world is still there. Hence the repetitive nature of the vision, which earlier commentators—preferring what they knew, that is, narratives that steadily advance—considered clumsy, but which certain commentators have now recognized as its fundamental design. After the destruction wrought by the opening of the first six seals of the book of the Lamb, a multitude cry with a loud voice: "Salvation to our God which sitteth upon the throne, and unto the Lamb" (7:10). After the destruction and death that follow the six trumpets of the seventh seal, great voices proclaim: "The kingdoms of this world are become the kingdoms of our Lord, and of his Christ" (11:15). When Michael and his angels defeat the dragon who is the Devil and Satan, a loud voice cries: "Now is come salvation, and strength, and the kingdom of our God, and the power of his Christ" (12:10). Other contests and judgments end in similar acclamations of triumph. The narrative seems to advance while standing still. The "great day of [the Lamb's] wrath is come" (6:17) already after the opening of the sixth seal, yet later in the work, after the sounding of the seventh trumpet of the seventh seal the twenty-four elders thank God, saying: "thy wrath is come" (11:18). And again, when the sixth seal is opened, all mountains and islands are "moved out of their places" (6:14); when Babylon is split asunder, every island again flees and the mountains are not to be found (16:20). If the sixth seal causes the sun to turn black, the moon to become as blood and the stars to fall to earth (6:12–13), the heavens appear to have been restored before the fourth angel sounds and a third part of the sun is smitten, along with a third part of the moon and of the stars (8:12), while the sun is still there to receive the wrath of God in the fourth plague (16:8).

The sequence of the vision is organized so as to alert us to the sense of this repetitiveness. Since heaven departs "as a scroll when it is rolled together" (6:14) yet sun, moon and stars reappear in later recountings, we are clearly being given partial glimpses, different angles of vision onto a single, fundamental strife. The story does move forward, but not through simple chronology. A seal releases Death, to whom power is given over a *fourth* part of

The Timing

---

the earth (6:8); a trumpet strikes a *third* part of the sun, the moon and the stars (8:12); the plagues destroy *everything* that needs destroying (chapter 16). God "shall wipe away all tears" from the eyes of those who have passed through the great tribulation (7:17); he "shall wipe away all tears" from the eyes of all those who find themselves in the new heaven and the new earth (21:4). The powerful and highly inventive form of the narrative invites us to read it as a series of developing ways of showing the victory of God over evil, as if we were peeling off layer after layer of the truth and seeing the Real behind reality more and more fully. As the images change while the tale told remains basically the same, we are drawn into seeing that so much of what is related concerns the present, the now of the reader in whatever century he reads.

2

And after all, so much of what we see in Revelation has, as many have pointed out, already happened. The successive battles against evil, were they not won when Jesus resisted the devil in the wilderness, when he renounced his own will in the place called Gethsemane, and when he submitted on the cross? On the cross, as Paul writes, "having spoiled principalities and powers, he made a shew of them openly, triumphing over them" (Colossians 2:15). In John's visions, the wrath of God continually falls on evil, and according to Paul we can see this now: "For the wrath of God is revealed (*apokalyptetai*) from heaven against all ungodliness and unrighteousness of men" (Romans 1:18). The *revelation* is already with us. Towards the end of his vision, John sees "the holy city, new Jerusalem, coming down from God out of heaven" (21:2), yet the Letter to the Hebrews tells all Christians, here and now: "ye are come unto mount Sion, and unto the city of the living God, the heavenly Jerusalem" (Hebrews 12:22). When the four angels are told not to hurt the earth and the sea till the servants of God have been "sealed" in their foreheads (7:3), we surely remember that God has already "sealed us, and given the earnest of the Spirit in our hearts" (2 Corinthians 1:22); that, like the Ephesians, after believing the gospel we "were sealed with that holy Spirit of promise" (Ephesians 1:13), by whom we were "sealed unto the day of redemption" (Ephesians 4:30).

One moment in Revelation seems designed to make us reflect on the unimaginable temporality into which we have been drawn. As I mentioned above, on only one occasion is John asked the meaning of what he sees, much to his confusion. In reading the explanation given by one of the elders: the multitude praising God are "they which came out of the great tribulation" (7:14), one should remember that in Matthew's gospel Jesus refers to a "great tribulation" to come (Matthew 24:21, 29), and to occur just prior to the Son of man descending "in the clouds of heaven with power and great glory" (v. 30). If, like John, we could see into heaven, we should realize that all future Christians through however much history remains are, for God, already there.

Caught up "in the Spirit," John lives briefly beyond our time, and sees (almost) what *is*. He cannot penetrate to what we can only conceive as the now of eternity, or as a time beyond the capacity of our mind, but he does see outside of time as we know it. Hence, surely, an expression that returns, with variations, as a kind of refrain. John wishes the seven churches grace and peace "from him which is, and which was, and which is to come" (1:4), and God presents himself with the same formula a few verses later. The order of time as we think it: past, present, and future, is changed so as to highlight the present, the everlasting presence of God. When Jesus then addresses John, however, he speaks to his earthly sense of time by way of contrast: "Write the things which thou hast seen, and the things which are, and the things which shall be hereafter" (1:19). The heavenly order returns when the elders thank the Lord God Almighty "which art, and wast" (11:17) for having taken to himself his great power, and when the angel pouring a plague on rivers and springs acknowledges the justice of God, "which art, and wast," in so judging (16:5). The absence of the future tense seems to imply that the vision has moved closer to the end of the world. The four living creatures nevertheless worship the God "which was, and is, and is to come" (4:8), perhaps to show, by this apparent anomaly, the impossibility of our understanding.

A hint of this other time that the work enables us to learn occurs in a further detail in John's presentation of Jesus: "Behold, he cometh with clouds; and every eye shall see him" (1:7). We *shall* see him, he has not yet come with clouds, but, at the same time, he is already coming. Eternity already presses on us, as a future present. And when Jesus alerts us to the end, he does not ask us to calculate when it will occur: he warns of its unpredictable suddenness. He tells the church in Sardis: "Be watchful," for if not "I will come on thee as a thief, and thou shalt not know what hour I will come upon thee" (3:2–3). Even more pointedly, he interrupts John's description of a great event so as to repeat his warning:

> And I saw three unclean spirits.... the spirits of devils ... *which* go forth unto the kings of the earth and of the whole world, to gather them to the battle of that great day of God Almighty. Behold, I come as a thief. Blessed *is* he that watcheth, and keepeth his garments, lest he walk naked, and they see his shame. And [they] gathered them together into a place called in the Hebrew tongue Armaggedon. (16:13–16)

I have quoted the passage at length because in a literary work the context is part of the meaning. Jesus intervenes just when we are probably asking ourselves when this "apocalyptic" battle will occur, so as to reorient our thinking, to tell us that we cannot know in advance. Or perhaps to advise us, if the battle is already won, is occurring around us, or is a future event, that his coming, whether into our lives now or into the whole world at the end of the present heaven and earth, is always unexpected. When Jesus says to the churches at the beginning (2:5, 16; 3:11) and repeatedly as the vision closes (22:7, 12, 20), "I come quickly (*tachy*)," we should remember that *tachy* can also imply suddenness. God is "ready to judge the quick and the dead," writes Peter (1 Peter 4:5); for James, "the judge standeth before the door" (James 5:9).

After speaking at length to his disciples about the sign of his coming and "the end of the world" (Matthew 24:3), Jesus tells them to "watch," and adds: "if the goodman of the house had known in what watch the thief would come, he would have watched" (v. 43). On his saying, in the course of the same teaching, "When ye therefore shall see the abomination of desolation, spoken of by Daniel the prophet, stand in the holy place," Matthew intervenes to address the reader: "whoso readeth, let him understand" (v. 15). Mark intervenes likewise in his account of the warning (Mark 13:14). I rather doubt that the evangelists are urging us to work out what this abomination of desolation may be and when it might occur. We cannot understand now, before the event; we are to understand it when it occurs, and shall do so if we obey the so frequently expressed brief command: "Watch."

3

Our time is open to infinity, which intervenes continually. And perhaps time is not a movement forward to the edge of a cliff at the end of the world: since the cross and resurrection we are already at the cliff's edge, and our time moves sideways along it.

The Timing

This sheds light on one of the simplest and most perplexing of all Jesus's commands: "Take . . . no thought for the morrow" (Matthew 6:34). His words acquire a specific meaning in Revelation. Our business is not, in Eliot's words, to "haruspicate or scry," to fix the date of the millennium or the capture of the beasts and the false prophet, but to watch. It might be objected that to concentrate so intently on the present empties the future and makes light of hope. Yet hope, by giving confidence in the future—not in what might happen but in God's purpose in all that happens—is precisely what makes it possible to take no thought for tomorrow. As soon as we begin to read Revelation, moreover, we meet, after the vision of Jesus with the candlesticks and the stars, not visionary images of supernatural events but the urgency, the call to action now, in the letters to the seven churches. The Christians at Ephesus and at Sardis are told to remember and to repent (2:5; 3:3), the church at Pergamos must also repent (2:16) as must the followers of "Jezebel" in the church in Thyatira (2:22), while the Laodiceans are to repent and to be zealous (3:19). Three of the churches are commended for their "patience" (endurance, *hypomonē*—2:2, 3, 19; 3:10); the idea returns in the phrase, "Here is the patience . . . of the saints," as a soberly realistic comment on the "apocalyptic" moments of the beast's war against the saints (13:10) and of his hour of judgement (14:12). The word occurs also in the middle of the "apocalyptic" warnings of Jesus in the Gospels: "he that shall endure (*hypomeinas*) unto the end, the same shall be saved" (Matthew 24:13; Mark 13:13). At the finish of each of the seven letters a promise is made "to him that overcometh." Why should Revelation begin with these letters to churches if not to remind us of their pressing need and ours, as a sign that we should read the rest of the work with this ever-present spiritual danger and need for exertion in mind? The letters do not constitute a prelude to Revelation, since the work is addressed in its entirety to the churches (22:16). Their members will hear or read the whole of John's vision with their own situation before them.

If the beginning of the work stresses the present, so does the end. We see the future, the new Jerusalem, the tree of life, a world without sun or night flooded with the light of the Lord God, and Jesus is still to "come quickly" (22:7, 12, 20). Yet the future tips over into the present through superb wordplay: "And the Spirit and the bride say, Come. And let him that heareth say, Come. And let him that is athirst come" (22:17). We say "come" to Jesus because he is not yet here "as he is" (1 John 3:2), but we also are invited to come, not later, but now. Jesus returns our word as a gift and repeats his own invitation while on earth: "If any man thirst, let him come unto me, and drink" (John 7:37). In its recurring presentness his offer echoes that already made in Isaiah: "Ho, every one that thirsteth, come ye to the waters" (Isaiah 55:1). The next words in Revelation are even more pointed: "And whosoever will, let him take the water of life freely." An angel has just shown John "a pure river of water of life" (22:1) flowing in a future world by the tree of life, from which the reader in every age is nevertheless encouraged to drink.

This focus on the reader's present should surely prompt us to see the images in Revelation as revealing, at least in the first instance, "things which are" (1:19). John's first vision of supernatural beings acting (other than worshipping and casting crowns before the throne) would seem to lead us in this direction. In chapter 6, it is stated explicitly that horsemen released by the opening of the first four seals travel the earth to bring death, by war, hunger, disease, and wild beasts (6:8). Death is already with us, those are its principal causes, and when we learn of the second horseman that his role is "to take peace from the earth, and that they should kill one another" (6:4), we surely realize that this concerns us, and that one of the sources of death is in

The Timing

ourselves, in our violence, as it has been since the disobedience of Adam and Eve. As others have seen, the horsemen are images of what is in us and around us. They and their horses are already everywhere, and our task is neither to project them into the end of the ages, nor to discard them as images once we think we have interpreted them. They are there to be meditated, as a powerful image of certain forces with which we must live, galloping and wreaking havoc.

The locusts in chapter 9 rise, in smoke resembling that of a great furnace, from the bottomless pit. The images of smoke darkening the sun and of an abyss that terrifies devils (Luke 8:31) suggest a nightmare, and the horror is compounded by the command they receive not to kill but to torment for five months with a torment like that of a scorpion. The nightmare thickens when they are described as having the shape of a horse, human faces, women's hair, and the teeth of lions, and as making a clatter like that of horses and chariots running into battle. But whom do they torment?—"those men which have not the seal of God in their foreheads" (9:4), who seek death, "and shall not find it" (v. 6). Is this, perhaps, the nightmare truth of unbelief, as heaven sees it for humans, the desperate and ugly reality of indifference or refusal, of the final hopelessness? If one wants to know what obdurate atheism amounts to, maybe one should contemplate the locusts.

The passage recalls the panic that follows the opening of the sixth seal in chapter 6, when those who feel "the wrath of the Lamb" (6:16), those for whom the sun and moon are disfigured, the stars fall, heaven disappears and earth becomes a chaos—for whom the whole world loses meaning—hide in caves and, despairing of escape, call on mountains to crush them. Once again, the images speak to now, and *seeing* them enables one to see the world as it will finally appear to anyone who refuses God's love and who realizes his error.

In observing the two beasts of chapter 13, we see the real face of evil and worldliness, which are part of our condition and are at home among us. The first does at least emerge from the sea, a place alien from us, as is the devil. The second, however, emerges from the earth, like Adam and like ourselves. To worship the beast (13:8) rather than God, to admire the way of the world, with all the "great wonders" (v. 13) it produces, to give oneself to it without reference to anything higher, is ultimately, in the eyes of God and to the eyes of his visionary, to adore a monster. The images of the beasts should remain with us to remind us what our culture, our science, our politics, and all our activities look like, not in themselves, not in the prodigious creativity that we exercise as creatures made in the image of a Creator God, but when we make them ends in themselves and turn them into idols.

In considering the most grotesque of all John's images, that of the "great whore" who appears in chapter 17, sitting on a beast and on "many waters" (17:1), we are led by the work itself to see in her a representation of power—she is "that great city, which reigneth over the kings of the earth" (17:18)—and of money: when she falls, it is "the merchants of the earth" who mourn (18.11). Or, more precisely, of power and money pursued for their own sake and adored. Here, too, to focus on the image is to see that worldly power employed and riches accumulated for no better reason than to glorify oneself are not glorious but monstrous, and will finally encounter a contrary Power of a different order, that of the Lamb (17:14), the unanswerable might of the most meek and destitute. We remember Hobbes's Leviathan; we should remember John's drunken whore.

Above all, to take in the image, as John does, is to look for what the image may suggest beyond what I or anyone else may say of it, beyond any error we may be fostering. It is to allow the image to speak, which it does more fully than the commentator.

The Timing

The harder one looks, moreover, the more one sees. Discussing the "woman clothed with the sun" of chapter 12, I suggested that the striking metaphors and lively narrative through which we perceive her can always offer more. Indeed, on reading that she "cried, travailing in birth, and pained to be delivered" (12:2), one recalls what Paul hears in the universe: "the whole creation groaneth and travaileth in pain" (Romans 8:22). One might then look again at this woman associated with the sun and the moon and wearing a crown, not of many stars but twelve, the number suggesting completeness. Having given birth to a child who is to rule all nations and who is the beginning of the new covenant and the new birth, she could well evoke the whole creation travailing to bring forth the new heaven and the new earth. She resembles the young woman in the Song of Songs, "fair as the moon, clear as the sun, majestic as the stars in procession" (6:10; the last expression seems closer to the sense than the King James translation). I suggested in my book *Bible and Poetry* that the woman of the Song, decked also with beautiful metaphors from so many aspects of the earthly creation, is the image, among other things, of nature perfected; she is herself "all fair," without a "spot" (4:7). Surrounded by an implausibly rich vegetation, she offers a glimpse of a new creation, of the new heaven and earth that the fabulous woman in Revelation is perhaps travailing to produce. Yet it is the fictive reality of both these female figures, who are more than powerful allegories, that asks to be contemplated. What should remain in the memory from Revelation is the visionary narrative of a woman crowned with stars pursued by a dragon.

In the preface to *Frankenstein* Mary Shelley writes that the central event, "however impossible as a physical fact, affords a point of view to the imagination for the delineating of human passions more comprehensive and commanding than any which the ordinary relations of existing events can yield." If one replaces "for the delineating of human passions" by, say, "for perceiving the reality of the world in which we find ourselves," one catches the sense of Revelation. By this vision John sees things as they are, and he witnesses their future consummation and renewal. Through him we see the fallen world, the rejection of God, the complicity with evil as grotesque nightmare. We see Jesus, the subject of the book, not yet as he is but with a clearer view: as awesome—his eyes "as a flame of fire" (1:14)—as at the transfiguration, at the one moment of vision granted to three of the disciples. We see him also as the Lamb, as love—from the very beginning as he "that loved us, and washed us from our sins in his own blood" (1:5)—a reminder of God's love and of the joy of salvation that prepares one for the horrors to come. The many songs and cries of praise that punctuate the narrative provide a view through to a kind of heavenly *now* opening beyond our own present.

4

Revelation is the perfect work to conclude the Bible. Commentators have pointed out that its own end refers continually to its beginning. The first verse is recalled in detail in the last chapter:

> The Revelation of Jesus Christ, which God gave unto him, to
> shew unto his servants things which must shortly come to
> pass; and he sent and signified it by his angel.... (1:1)

> ... the Lord God of the holy prophets sent his angel to shew
> unto his servants the things which must shortly be done. (22:6)

The repetition is not awkward; it makes a point. The promises in the letters to the seven churches are likewise remembered as the work closes. For example, Jesus's announcement that he will give "the morning star" to whoever overcomes (2:28) returns when he reveals that he is himself "the bright and morning star" (22:16). His pledge to retain the name of such a person in "the book of life" (3:5) returns in the reference to "the Lamb's book of life" (21:27). Another assurance given, "I will write upon him ... my new name" (3:12), is recalled when John understands that Christians will have Jesus's name "in their foreheads" (22:4). The work mirrors the whole Bible as a narrative of prophecy and fulfillment. It constitutes, it seems, a kind of literary echo of God, of Jesus, as "Alpha and Omega, the beginning and the ending" (1:8), an expression repeated in different forms at the beginning of the book (1:11, 17; 2:8) and that is itself repeated at the end: "I am Alpha and Omega, the beginning and the end" (21:6; 22:13). As a piece of inspired writing, Revelation shows in its form what it has to say, with deftness and originality.

Its relation to the Bible as a whole is equally final and eminently satisfying. Like all New Testament texts it unfolds as a palimpsest, rewriting any number of Old Testament passages, modifying them in a further perspective, replaying them with a difference, according to the innovative (as opposed to inert) repetition at the heart of Christianity. But Revelation is also the last and complete gathering, the reinterpretation of prophecies leading to a new and extended vision of the "last things" and of the world to come.

And if its end repeats its beginning, as the end of the Bible it repeats, very precisely, the Bible's beginning. It returns to the Creation in the vision of the New Jerusalem. The announcement that "there shall be no night" (22:5) reverses the creation of night in Genesis 1:5. The absence of sun and moon (21:23) does away with the "two great lights" of Genesis 1:16. The absence of light (22:5) removes the very first thing created (Genesis 1:3). It returns to the Fall when the woman giving birth to a child destined to conquer the dragon who is the devil (chapter 12) fulfills the prophecy concerning the seed of Eve (Genesis 3:15). The fact that, in the New Jerusalem, "there shall be no more death" (21:4) annuls the punishment imposed on Adam after the Fall (Genesis 3:19), while the fact that "there shall be no more curse" (22:3) perhaps removes, among other things, the curse on the ground that likewise followed the Fall (Genesis 3:17). The presence of the "tree of life" (22:2, 14), just when the Bible is about to conclude the Christian revelation, finally reopens "the way of the tree of life" (Genesis 3:24) that, after the Fall, cherubim and a flaming sword made impassable. The creation of "a new heaven and a new earth" (21:1) returns one to the very first words of the Bible: "In the beginning God created the heaven and the earth," so as to reveal not the utter difference of the new but its creative repetition of the old. Revelation, by a great feat of inspired imagination and writing, rounds off and opens up.

As a summary and a completion of the Bible, Revelation also draws it towards vision. The Bible ends, not in propositions but in images, in a world of angels pouring out plagues and of beasts with seven heads or with the voice of a dragon, of a woman with an eagle's wings, of a city of precious stones. A final reinforcing of the fact that the Bible is not a European or Western treatise. That the strangeness of Christianity is part of its timelessness and its unceasing untimeliness.

SCRIPTURE INDEX

Scripture Index

Revelation (*continued*)

1:9–10	78
1:10	73, 74, 80, 82, 83, 89
1:11	80, 112
1:12	71, 74
1:12–13	73
1:13	78, 89
1:14	111
1:14–16	89
1:17	112
1:19	80, 93, 103–4, 107
1:20	86–87, 95
2–3	79
2:2	106
2:3	106
2:5	105, 106
2:7	21
2:8	112
2:16	105, 106
2:17	23
2:18	89
2:19	106
2:22	106
2:26–27	93
2:28	112
3:1	81
3:2–3	104
3:3	106
3:5	112
3:10	106
3:11	105
3:12	112
3:19	106
4	86, 92
4:1	73, 79, 90
4:1–2	81
4:2	82, 90
4:3	90
4:4	79
4:6	90
4:7	90, 92
4:8	81, 92, 104
4:8–9	79
4:10	79
5	88
5:1	73
5:2	73
5:6	73
5:11	73
6	88
6:1	73
6:4	85, 107
6:8	102, 107
6:12–13	101
6:12–14	90
6:14	101
6:16	108
6:17	101
7:3	103
7:10	101
7:14	76, 103
7:17	102
8:12	101, 102
9	108
9:3	90
9:4	108
9:5	90
9:6	108
9:7–10	90
10:4	80, 98
10:6	100
10:7	96, 97
10:10	98
11:8	97
11:15	93, 96, 101
11:17	104
11:18	101
12	113
12:1	81, 93, 94, 91
12:1–2	93
12:2	110
12:3	91, 93
12:4	94
12:5	93
12:7	97
12:10	101
12:10–12	94
12:17	97
13:2	91
13:8	109
13:10	106
13:13	109
14:8	76
14:10	76
14:12	106
14:15	76–77

Scripture Index

120

Scripture Index

Richard E. Myers Lectures

———————

Fully Alive: The Apocalyptic Humanism of Karl Barth
STANLEY HAUERWAS

More Things in Heaven and Earth: Shakespeare, Theology,
and the Interplay of Texts
PAUL S. FIDDES

Making the World Over: Confronting Racism, Misogyny,
and Xenophobia in U.S. History
R. MARIE GRIFFITH

Printed in the USA
CPSIA information can be obtained
at www.ICGtesting.com
LVHW091226151223
766489LV00004B/441

9 780813 950532